THE
TRIAL

THE
TRIAL

Rev. Rickey McDonald

Library of Congress Control Number: 2025918920

ISBN: 979-8-89228-783-8   (Paperback)
ISBN: 979-8-89228-786-9   (eBook)

Printed in the United States of America

CAUTION

Readers, you are forewarned and above all asked to exercise extreme caution while reading this book. You who have weak stomachs are also cautioned: this book will take you places you have never been and will show you sights you have never seen before.

Some of the things that you will mentally see and physically read, which are stated and proven in this book, have caused allergies to spontaneously disappear, illnesses to dissipate, cancerous diseases to be gone and become untraceable, and much, much more. Yes, many things, such as those just stated and which I call Infection in this book, have a CURE.

This age–old story and court case is now revealed for the first and only time ever. The trial you are about to embark upon has some very hideous sections. Some of the things you will read are incomprehensible, and the worst part of all is: This story truly happened.

Without further ado,

With forewarning,

Prepare yourself,
and above all:

EXPECT THE
UNEXPECTED!

Brief Overview

The future of the entire world is weighed in the balance of justice today. Those being charged with these horrifically gruesome criminal acts and/or omissions willfully committed both separate and corporate acts, thereby making this not only a single but a corporate crime and trial.

The acts and/or omissions have had an everlasting effect on the world. These actions and/or omissions caused an infection. Yes, an infection of such magnitude that the world never knew previously and from which it has never recovered.

Though these are separate and corporate crimes, the crime committed by each defendant, separate from the other, carries an **equal punishment.** Therefore, it is the duty of the court to hear and try these defendants for their acts, actions, and/or omissions at the same time.

This case is being held in satisfaction of The Law, spoken and understood by each defendant. Sentences and/or pardons given are in the hands of **THE** Supreme Court Justice, **God Almighty**, and His judgment rendered is final and leaves no room for appeal. Any sentence imposed will be enforced!

Two of these defendants tried to hide the truth (their criminal actions) and tried to keep their acts, actions, and/or omissions from being discovered by **The Truth.** However, today is their day. They will be afforded the opportunity – if they can – to justify their individual and corporate acts and/or omissions. They will have the chance to prove that he, she, or they: 1) did not commit the crime, 2) were forced to commit the crime, or 3) did not know it was a crime.

Evidence will be used to prove or disprove that the charges against these culprits are justified and truthful. The judge will pay attention to everything shown, said, and submitted, whether it is physical, visual, or verbal evidence, before He decides for or against each of the accused.

The **Trial Transcripts** are only available within this book. Again, I must inform you that the facts concerning this case are both hideous and incomprehensible. Nevertheless, they are true. However, as we all know, there are two sides to every story.

Gentlemen, ladies, boys, and girls: wait and wonder no longer why this is and always has been one of the most highly acclaimed trials ever held and recorded. This trial is one of, if not **the** most talked–about trials, even in today's day and age. It is a widely known fact that this case is the greatest recorded event ever to have been handed down from generation to generation.

Yet, this Trial, for the most part, has never been heard or told in the way I am about to tell it. So, sit back and get comfortable. What you are about to read is unimaginable, unbelievable, and undoubtedly **The Greatest Trial** ever shown, told, or known to man.

DEDICATIONS

I dedicate this book to:

1. The Lord, Jesus Christ, who **is <u>my</u>** Savior.

2. My loving wife, who tirelessly read, reread, helped to edit, prayed, and gave up the computer many times so I could continue writing these books.

3. My Mother. Who gave up having and doing as she desired so I could have **A Better Life.**

4. A special dedication: to my dearly missed and never–to–be–replaced Grandfather. This was a man I can truly say was like King David, meaning a man after God's own heart. **Pop**, you know, no doubt, how much you meant and will always mean to me. Thank **YOU**, Reverend Noble G.W. McDonald, for honoring me with the ability to see Jesus through and in you!

FORWARD

Section One: You will find questions, thoughts, ideas, and suggestions within these chapters. They contain personal thoughts, suggestions, and ideas that I claim to be associated with statements made. Some thoughts, ideas, and suggestions will be more than mere statements as they will be backed by Biblical Scripture or other references.

Section Two: You will read what I'm calling "Trial Transcripts" of this age–old, highly controversial, misinterpreted, and far too often misunderstood trial that will state and prove that criminal acts, actions, and/or omissions took place.

As this trial starts to unfold, consider the following facts. The defendants named and charged in this case were not strangers. They lived in the same area of town, so to speak. They saw and talked to each other daily. No, these defendants were not strangers, and yet, in a way, they were.

Let's start by getting to know something about the place where the crime happened, and then those involved. This is a scene easily recognized and very familiar to most. This **Trial** is about –

1   A Married Couple (with children),

2   A Special Tree,

3   An Outcast and Outsider,

4   A Beautiful Garden,

5   Food "Fruit," (or was it?)

6   Truth and Obedience, and Lies and Deception,

7   A Husband and Father, and Wife and Mother.

It's unbelievable, and yet true!

Who are these criminals? What did they do that was so bad? Could or did they really change the entire world? Judge for yourself and then decide if pardons or sentences handed down by THE Supreme Court Justice were justifiable. If you do not agree, consider this: neither you nor I can give or take a life justifiably.

You're about to meet the defendants. They have allegedly committed, independently and corporately, the greatest criminal acts this world has ever known. Those being charged are:

1. **Eve** – Mother and Wife to Adam.

2. **Adam** – Father and Husband to Eve.

3. An outsider notoriously and commonly called the evil one, the father of lies, the angel of light, satan, Lucifer, and **the serpent** (to name a few of his aliases).

This third defendant has a criminal past. He was formally charged, tried, convicted, and sentenced for criminal misconduct and unworthiness in a trial similar to this one.

The third defendant not only took an active part in this crime, but also willingly participated in the criminal offenses. Therefore, if this defendant is found guilty of acts, actions, and/or omissions involving this case, he will be recognized and declared a habitual (repeat) offender. Considering he was formerly charged, tried, and adjudicated a criminal, it is easy to hypothesize he will more than likely lie, as he has done before[1].

This trial is about three defendants and how they willingly chose to **do their own thing**. They knew not to commit the crime. They heard the warning issued, and they chose to disobey. Thus, if they are found guilty, they will reap the consequences of disobedience for their crime.

Two of these defendants will learn what it means to be an outcast and outsider, and what it feels like to be a criminal for the first time.

Together, these defendants committed willful (note the word **willful**) misconduct resulting in a crime that not only affected these defendants but also cursed all of humanity forever. Yes, every single living, breathing, walking, talking human being still pays for the act, acts, actions, and/or omissions that each knowingly and willfully joined in on and deliberately committed.

---

[1] **The former and first trial ever held and heard tried defendant number three as the sole perpetrator. His unadulterated lying, deceiving, and cunning ways, his "word construction" (further expounded upon in my book called The Genesis Effect), led thousands of innocent beings to permanent, utter, and total death (better understood as permanent banishment) and the destruction of the beings who followed and believed him.**

You will also read how these culprits were able to change the entire Earth and God's Greatest Creation, **man**kind, eternally. What they did as independent agents and as a corporate body caused and allowed the serpent to steal their eternal (salvation) life. That eternal salvation was not only stolen from them, but was stolen from those who followed them through conception and birth. How, you may ask? It is due to their **free will**.

What I mean by their **free will**, and how it has and still affects us, is this: Each had the ability to choose, to do what was correct and not prohibited by God, meaning not to touch or (eat) partake of the forbidden tree or its fruit. Each individually and willingly disregarded the warnings of God, which caused us to be infected with the disease known as **SIN**.

I believe the contents of this book will be enlightening and informative, especially for individuals having an open mind and a willing heart to accept what could have been.

My desire is to entice you to consider and believe that this trial actually happened. You may know this story well; it's been told and retold generation after generation. Even so, please take your time reading, for no doubt the information to which you're about to be exposed, you will never see or hear anywhere else, in quite this way, ever again. This Trial in and of itself had and still has the greatest impact on the entire world around us. So much attention surrounded this trial that, to date, there has never been a trial to reach such a magnitude nor be its equal.

ATTENTION:
ONE AND ALL

Not everything in this book exists,
at least not as far as records show or record.

Now sit back, relax, open your mind, and enjoy

THE TRIAL

Opening notes

Though I most likely do not know you, I want to extend an opportunity for you **to know** the same God that Adam, Eve, and I know. He is the same God today as He was when He created all that exists. I am offering, if you do not have it, **salvation** through the shed blood of God's Son, Jesus. If you will take a moment and come to know Him on a more personal level, possibly for the first time, then all you need to do is what the scripture says, and HE will live within you forevermore. **Romans 10:9** says, **"That <u>if thou shalt confess with thy mouth the Lord</u> Jesus, <u>and shalt believe in thine heart that God hath raised him</u> from the dead, thou shalt be saved."**

Just do what is underlined and you will have the chance to live eternally with God, with Jesus, possibly with family members who have gone before you, and with the entire heavenly host. However, there are some prerequisites. **First**, <u>you must come to realize</u> that you are a sinner from birth, and then, when you do what Romans 10:9 says, you will become a New Creature[2] through Christ Jesus.

Have you ever thought or imagined what this world would be like if God had not sent His **ONLY** Begotten Son into the world? All of humanity would be lost, and there would be no way **to know** God or the peace that He gives and provides to those who believe in and on Him. What a chaotic mess we would live in and suffer through without having or knowing The Hope of Eternal Life, who is none other than Jesus Christ.

Our souls could not contain all the evil that is in the world. Our minds could not fathom what peace, hope, joy, and everlasting love are. BUT GOD, being merciful, as He is, Sent THE Ultimate Sacrifice.

---

[2]   **2 Corinthians 5:17 "<u>Therefore if any man be in Christ, he is a new creature: old things are passed away; behold, all things are become new.</u>"**

Though Adam lost his and posterity's birthright in and to the Garden of Eden, Jesus came as the Second Adam[3], thereby regaining that which was lost. That is what Jesus said He came here for, "… **to seek and to save[4] that which was lost**." Now, rest assured that if you have done what the scripture says in Romans 10:9, you are saved, and you will live eternally with God.

With The Foundation laid, the scene set, prayer offered to and for you, it is now time to go forward. Let's see what God has to say through and throughout this (HIS) book,

THE TRIAL

---

[3]   **1 Corinthians 15:45 "…The first man Adam was made a living soul; the last Adam was made a quickening spirit."**

[4]   **Luke 19:10 "For the Son of Man is come to seek and to save that which was lost."**

1

THE FOUNDATION

It is common knowledge that a building does not stand or support itself without first having the required foundation on which to build its strength and stability. Therefore, I start by building, or as stated in Genesis 1:1 by *"creating"* (establishing), the foundation so you can become better acquainted with the accusations; the accused; and the criminal acts (individual and/or corporate), actions, and/or omissions that have been brought before the honorable court. What is my reasoning? This will afford a vicarious firsthand experience of what could have taken place and has not been recorded. Additionally, this foundation offers a better understanding of events that did happen and were recorded, as well as things that were overlooked in this story that have been told for ages.

> First, and in no particular order, you will see what the two defendants possessed and were willing to give up:

> A marvelous garden, containing all the essential elements and nutrients ever wanted or needed

> Flowers in full bloom daily, varied in color, shape, size, etc.

> Birds singing tranquil songs all day

> A luminous, climate–controlled residence where they could, and did, feel relaxed at all times

> Food in abundance, everywhere and at any time; each could be touched, held, eaten, admired, and enjoyed without limitation or restriction

> Total peace, joy, and love.

BUT these created and perfectly formed creatures did not desire to live in Paradise any longer, or is that how it really was? This Paradise was designed just for them, and yet the splendor of this place, and all that it contained, was not enough to keep them satisfied. (Who would not want to live where life was perfect all the time? "I would! Pick me. Pick me," I can hear myself saying.) These two never needed better, for there is nothing better than God Himself, and He came down daily to visit.

The Garden of Eden was the most beautiful place ever created by God on earth; it was and has always remained the best. If you have the best, then anything other would, by definition, be less. Let's look at this idea another way. Do you remember the second–place winners of competitions? It is, however, easy to remember first–place winners because they were the best in a particular competition, winning both the title and recognition. Second–place winners are rarely remembered. They are paid less and receive less because they did not win.

Yes, Adam and Eve had the best, and as the story goes, they were not satisfied. At first, they were, but later, when the enemy came and started befriending Eve, he gained her confidence through confusion. If the enemy (the serpent, as he's called in Genesis) was going to take what God had given them, he had to use extreme caution. Adam and Eve were not stupid; they knew that God created them, and it was God who said what was and was not allowed in the Garden of Eden. How hard could it have been for Adam to take control of the situation before it got out of hand? I think he could have done it easily. In fact, the Word of God (the Bible) says **they** had **dominion**[1], meaning they had total control, yet Adam failed to do his duty. Let's consider the word dominion.

---

[1] **Genesis 1:26** "And <u>God said</u>, Let us make man in our image, after our likeness: and **<u>let them have dominion</u>** over the fish of the sea, and over the fowl of the air, and over the cattle, and over all the earth, and over every creeping thing that creepeth upon the earth."

Total dominion was given to Adam and Eve (**Genesis 1:26**). Dominion for Adam and Eve is different than what dominion means for us today. God gave dominion (authority, right, duty, responsibility) to Adam, and he was to share this dominion with his wife, Eve. We have the same power, but in a more limited form. When Adam and Eve were given dominion, they had no sin in their lives. Until sin entered them, they were perfect. Adam was given the job of naming all the animals (another of God's creations), and he named them anything he desired. Though we can give animals names, we do not have the same dominion Adam had in the beginning.

Dominion was given specifically and freely to Adam and Eve. It didn't cost them anything, but today we pay for dominion because Adam and Eve chose to disobey God's commandments. We are now subject to sin or infection, as you will read. Their choice will continue to cost mankind forever, but fortunately, we have the cure. That cure is none other than Jesus, who also made a choice: to leave the splendor of heaven to suffer in the form of man, knowing full well He would be sacrificed (crucified) in our place for Adam's and Eve's disobedience and our sins.

God made this cure simple to understand, but there are those who cannot grasp the implications of this ageless "story." You can start by following the footnotes. They are intended to stimulate (your) spiritual growth. Scripture references are from the King James Version (KJV) of the Bible, unless otherwise noted. Some verses will be quoted while others may be only mentioned, thereby affording you the opportunity to investigate them and render your own decision.

This book is not geared toward seminary students, bishops, evangelists, preachers, etc. It is, however, intended to be a tool for those desiring to know, realize, and believe there is more to the book of Genesis than what lies on the surface. This is life, and it all started "in the beginning."

We know a house cannot stand without support, also known as a foundation. This chapter is a small segment of the foundation that I believe, on which I stand, and which I intend to show to those who bought and/or read this book. The real twist to this book is at the end, and it continues into the other books in this series.

2

Order / Sequence

Book 1
THE TRIAL
(including) Trial Transcripts

This book is the first part of a trilogy.
The names of the other books are:

Book 2
"The Genesis Effect"

Book 3
"The Blood Sealing Covenant"

There are other books that will follow in this "Redemption Series"

Some books have already begun the writing process, but they have not yet reached the point of publication.

Keep looking for my name and grab your copy so you can tell family and friends about each new title.

All of the books in the "trilogy" stem from the first three chapters of Genesis, but other scripture verses may also be included. Get a copy of every book in the "Redemption Series"

Thoughts, Suggestions, and Comments

These books are based on my thoughts, some suggestions, and several ideas that are mine alone. Do not allow the twists and turns to throw you off balance. Flow with the ride. Should you find yourself at odds with my thinking or statements, make an effort to consider my perspective. Then, if you still clash with something I've said, feel free to contact me at Rev83157@GMail.com. I will respond to any legitimate discussion.

Do not feel as though you need to read the entire book in your first sitting. Read at a comfortable pace. Revisit what you read, and yes, there may be some controversial complexities to this case (story). I firmly believe that if you devote enough time and thought and use the footnotes provided, a Bible and a Bible dictionary, you will come to realize this trial really took place. Above all, enjoy this purposely thought–provoking book.

We must go back to the beginning, back to the place where the defendants committed the criminal acts with which they are being charged and tried. I do not have actual transcripts in my possession. Neither do I claim to have firsthand knowledge of, experience of, nor notes from this trial. This case is developed in its present form and taken from the first three chapters of Genesis, the first book of the Holy Bible.

I do, however, have enough confidence to believe you will find this trial did take place, and it happened "in the beginning" – when there was no need for time.

3

TRIAL PREPARATIONS

There is a lot of work that goes into establishing a trial, referencing trials in our day and time. Many long, tiring hours are spent collecting evidence to prove and disprove allegations. Trials are hard to win, for both the prosecution and the defense. They are complicated, expensive, and time-consuming. It is common and necessary that there be (but not necessarily in the following order):

> A person, or persons, accused of a crime.

> Evidence. Allegations may be used, but for the most part, physical and circumstantial forms of evidence are disclosed.

> Criminal charges, or an indictment (a written form or document) used against those who are accused.

> Attorneys, prosecution, and defense. They are allotted equal opportunity (most of the time) to prove or disprove allegations made in the court, to a jury (if needed), and to defendants who are in the courtroom.

> The indictment, or formal charging document, reads something like: "Joe Doe, on or about January 1st, 1001 in the year of our Lord, did…." The indictment continues from that point on with other necessary allegations and information.

Consider the word "**did**"

It means someone is charged with the attempt to or they have carried out (completed) a criminal act. The implication being that the charge is a fact or will be factually proven.

This is what the prosecution claims, alleges, and shows as criminal misconduct, according to which the accused is charged and tried. These allegations will hopefully be proved through supporting evidence and/or witness testimony. Evidence is to be presented to support any and all accusations made. Allegations are then brought before and heard by the court having authority (jurisdiction) to rule on the particular case. Allegations are supposed to be truthful. Sometimes they are fabricated to keep the accused from being released to commit another crime or flee before s/he is tried.

Allegations are verbally introduced and read in front of a defendant or defendants, a jury (if needed), the presiding judge, and any spectators attending or who are in the courtroom.

The accused – in our day and time – has the right to competent representation, or defense counsel. Counsel's responsibility is to clarify all charges and then prepare a valid argument against these charges. In our day, we have what Adam and Eve did not: an attorney. Attorneys are trained in legal matters, which concern the judicial system and legal jargon (wording), to defend the accused with due diligence. Neither defense counsel nor a defendant has an obligation to prove innocence. It is, in my opinion, important to have all the evidence possible to disprove all accusations made against the accused.

Prosecutors, judicially speaking, bear the burden of proof. Prosecutors are to prove, as best as they can, the allegations made against the accused in and before a court (and jury) when deciding innocence or guilt. In most cases, both sides are allowed to present witnesses who will prove or disprove the allegations and evidence to render a fair and truthful decision.

This trial is different from any you have ever seen, about which you may have read, or in which you might have been a participant.

This trial – unlike any other – had an animal as part of and party to criminal acts and/or omissions alleged and tried.

Let us start with the following facts. Those being accused were friendly with each other. Two of the three accused were husband and wife. Their first meeting caused great excitement and inquisitiveness. The splendor that lay before them was truly amazing.

Everything considered necessary existed and was without restriction, except one; their habitat was filled with various trees, flowers, animals, etc. Their abode was astonishingly gorgeous. Yet complacency was their new close friend.

The owner of their abode asked only for compliance as payment (rent). They lived in ecstasy, which was a wedding gift from the GodFather. Dissatisfaction with their luminous wedding gift would be a greater loss than they could ever have imagined.

One defendant, unbeknownst to the others, was a convicted criminal. Yes, one of the accused committed the first and greatest criminal act ever recorded. That was case number one. It was settled quickly and permanently!

Allow your mind to be free and receptive as this trial unfolds. My goal is to provide information that, when examined, will help you grow to a deeper and more spiritual understanding of this age–old story. I'd dare say it has never been told like this. So, I say

"EXPECT
THE
UNEXPECTED!"

4

THOUGHTS AND FACTS

The Garden of Eden was impregnable. Like God's Word, it was structurally sound; it could not be penetrated by any outside force or power! It was vulnerable only from within. It had to be an inside job to take control of the Garden of Eden.

I am persuaded of this: while living in the Garden of Eden, Adam and Eve had seemingly unanswerable questions.

Questions like: "Why is it hard to live like this here?" "Is the serpent telling the truth?" and "Is God keeping the tree of knowledge of good and evil, the fruit from us? If He is, why?"

Why have I said this? Well, if I'm going to ask or state questions, it should be logical that I also answer the statement or question posed, right? Here's the answer to the seemingly odd statements I made concerning the thoughts of Adam and Eve.

I believe all that God's Word says. Paradise would have been their home forever if they simply kept doing what they had been doing before they – eventually – allowed the serpent to twist or confuse them. Why am I saying them? It was their blatant disregard for God and His commandments, and because of their reasoning and choices, that we suffer as we do every day. If they had believed God would punish them for their opposition, they would have stayed in perfect harmony, in the love, joy, and peace that He created them for the sinless Adam and Eve. Their offspring would have remained sinless. They had everything in Paradise, yet they grew discontent because they were not allowed to have one thing – the one thing that would eventually destroy them and their relationship with the GodFather.

Adam was the one who walked and talked with God during the cool of the day. It was his responsibility to discuss God's instructions with Eve. They chose, however, to listen to and obey their flesh – just like we do daily – instead of being trustworthy and obedient children. What caused them to make the decision they did, which they knew would ultimately violate God's directives? Free will or freedom of choice. They could choose to obey or disobey. They used their free will to do their own thing.

Scripturally, proof exists that Adam discussed God's edicts with Eve. The proof is in the words she spoke to the serpent. Because Eve demonstrated her knowledge of God's commands, God had the right and the obligation to execute the penalties and punishments that would be imposed if they disobeyed.

Yes, friend, Eden could only be penetrated at the point of its weakest link: Man (Adam) or Woman (Eve). This is how the Garden became infected with sin, what we call "the fall of man." For the snake (Adam's name for the serpent) to have what he longed for – the destruction of God's perfect creation – the two hand–formed beings had to allow the serpent's whisperings to penetrate their minds, their souls, and their hearts. They were created to know and show love. When the evil one finally infiltrated their minds, perfection was forever changed. We would still be captives, with a ransom continually in effect for our safe return, had Jesus not freely chosen to leave the splendor of heaven, take the form and knowledge of His first creation, man, and willingly choose to die for the sins our ancestors committed (as well as ours and those of our progeny).

It was the <u>wrong type of love</u> that caused Adam to willfully, blatantly, and intentionally sin. Adam longed for a relationship with Eve more than he did for his best friend and Creator. That newfound love **was evil!** Yet it was love, good love, that God showed us in consenting to and allowing His only begotten Son to come, live, and die for sin.

We sorrowfully inherit sin through conception and birth. As newborns, we do not have the choice to accept it or reject it. As part of our ancestors' actions, it has infected us. But God's love can create perfection within us, as it did within the defendants of this book. God affords the entire world, at some point in time, an opportunity to see His love in action. It's also easily gleaned through reading the Word of God. He even gives those who truly want to know Him better the ability to enter into a closer, more intimate relationship with Him. It is all due to the love Jesus has shown us, given to us, and sacrificed for us. Do you have and use that love?

If Adam and Eve had not disobeyed the plainly spoken directives issued as a warning, we wouldn't suffer as we do for their disobedience. Their blatant disregard has caused us to suffer for the choices they made, and we suffer even more than is necessary due to the disobedient, sinful things we ourselves do.

Purposeful disobedience to God, parents, or those in authority usually carries a penalty. Why? No one likes to be punished, even when we know we have done wrong. But when we go against the grain, we endure the consequences. Life, in its unfolding, has consequences, even if consequences are delayed. Adam and Eve knew something would happen because of their choices, and yet they did what they wanted to do.

What are some of the ways we suffer for their disobedience? One I'm sure most women immediately recognize is in childbirth.

Scripturally speaking, one of Eve's punishments was <u>increased pain in and during childbirth</u>. Neither Adam nor Eve ever suffered from being too hot or too cold, nor did Adam ever sweat from working, until he, rather they, disobeyed what God said: "…in the beginning…."

Have you ever wondered what would have happened if Adam had chosen not to accept and/or to eat the forbidden fruit? Or what would have happened if Adam had stopped Eve from touching, looking at, holding, and partaking of it? What would have happened if Adam had told the serpent never to talk to Eve? Because of Adam's God given authority over the entire Garden of Eden, Adam could have done just that! What would have happened if he had used his authority and commanded the serpent never to have eye contact, make gestures to, or speak with, etc., himself or Eve ever? What if?

God gave His commander, Adam, control over the Garden of Eden. Instructions from God to Adam were passed on to Eve. Adam did this, as we can see from Eve's response to the serpent in verse one of Genesis chapter 3.

Eve tells[2] the serpent what they are and are not allowed to eat. God never said, "Do not sit under the forbidden tree" (for shade, to relax), nor anything of the sort. God plainly said, "Do not **touch or**

---

2   **Genesis 3:1–5**

   1   Now the serpent was more subtil than any beast of the field which the LORD God had made. And he said unto the woman, Yea, **hath God said, Ye shall not eat of every tree of the garden?**

   2   And the woman said unto the serpent, **We may eat of the fruit of the trees of the garden:**

   3   **But of the fruit of the tree which is in the midst of the garden, God hath said, Ye shall not eat of it, neither shall ye touch it, lest ye die.**

   4   And the serpent said unto the woman, Ye shall not surely die:

   5   For God doth know that in the day ye eat thereof, then your eyes shall be opened, and ye shall be as gods, knowing good and evil

eat" from the forbidden tree. This proves Adam did give Eve the dos and don'ts issued by God.

I believe their next thoughts could have been, "The serpent might be right about this tree and the forbidden fruit the tree seems to hold, according to what the serpent says."

Each day Eve thought and watched, not recognizing the identity of the snake[3] as he touched, picked, and ate – in front of them – the forbidden fruit. The facial expressions they saw and the sounds they heard while the snake enjoyed the fruit told them how good it must be, so they wondered what a piece would be like. Eve, after watching and listening, found herself saying: "I want some!"

She thinks, "I've watched intently, time and time again, as he eats this fruit, and I have not seen any changes. Let me try it **once** to see what happens, if anything at all. Is he right? Is he wrong? I wish I knew for sure."

Eve's last comment, "I wish I knew for sure," shows the seed of doubt was planted and watered daily by the serpent's words. That process initiated the doubt whether Adam's words to her were from God and caused her to question the truthfulness of her husband.

> ChatGPT Quote:
> "Doubt is often considered a starting point for critical thinking and the search for knowledge or clarity, rather than the beginning of confusion."
> November 15, 2025.

---

3   He was not a "snake" [reptile] as we have come to know snakes. His name and description, when he was a heavenly angel, was Lucifer.

The Word of God says, "God is not the author[4] of confusion." So, the confusion (the doubt, if you will) Eve suffered from did not come from her God–given ability, but from her free will to think critically and to decide, which was her God–given right to do. This free will can also be called curiosity or desire, and it was the **"desire to know"** about something identified as not being in her (our) best interest. So, I say, "Wrong, wrong, wrong, Eve!"

It will soon be apparent why this trial was necessary, and the reason for the magnitude and harshness of the punishments that were handed down. God allowed these criminal acts, actions, and omissions to be written on scrolls, read before scribes and Pharisees, and reviewed and discussed by theologians, all for one purpose: So we could learn from the mistakes made by Adam and Eve. You will see why each criminal did not receive the death penalty, yet they received the Death Penalty.

The man and woman, Adam and Eve, loved one another. In the beginning, they obeyed all **the** commandments in accordance with the GodFather's directives. Each willingly complied with the directives spoken to them, which were for their personal health, welfare, and safety.

One commandment I believe they enjoyed, as we do, was to "… be fruitful and multiply...." Usually, there's a nine–month period of time (cycle) before a child is born. Children are the result of being fruitful and multiplying. This is what Adam and Eve's children did in providing grandchildren.

---

[4]   1 Corinthians 14:33
  "For God is not the author of confusion, but of peace, as in all churches of the saints."

This process of enlarging and multiplying will continue until the end of time. As this couple was instructed, we continue and enjoy the act and actions of being fruitful and multiplying, whether through adoption or by natural birth.

We love having someone carry on our family name, heritage, and traditions. Why do we love the "natural process" of multiplying? Because it was meant to be "GOOD" and God (instituted, allowed) ordained this from "the beginning" of time. Adam and Eve had the best of everything, but they chose to take their free will in a direction that would cause them more heartache and pain than they ever could have imagined.

One condition from which Adam and Eve suffered, we also suffer from. It's called **complacency**. Why are we so complacent? Why are we never satisfied? When I say never satisfied, I'm referring to the fact that if we were truly satisfied, we wouldn't want more or better because what we have satisfies us. It's "good" enough.

While Adam and Eve lived in the Garden of Eden, the GodFather expected one thing. It was a simple request and easy to fulfill. In no way was it harmful, unbearable, or overly burdensome, and yet they could not, for some unknown reason, perform the task. The one thing God wanted was pleasing, and it made Him happy: total obedience.

Obedience is easy if we allow ourselves to be humble and trust what God asks of us. When you think about it, we expect our children or employees to be obedient. Like Adam and Eve, our children can accomplish these small, and usually effortless tasks… until complacency or rebellion enters their heart and mind. So, why are we as hard as we are on our children for disobeying when it's Adam and Eve's fault? We expect "the Good" inside of us to change a pattern that was established by our forefathers, Adam and Eve, long before we were considered, conceived, and born to our parents.

The "Good and Evil" inside the forbidden fruit that hung on the Tree of Knowledge of Good **And** Evil was vital to the well–being, the health, and the welfare of **all of** humanity. Adam and Eve were only created with GOOD in them. Their decision to be disobedient children – to God – caused the infection (sin) we endure every day of our lives. The only way to get the cure for our inherited infection is by accepting the gift of eternal life through salvation, which only comes by and through the shed blood of Jesus, the Christ, the Only Son of God who lived here in the flesh.

This story, as it has been penned, has many twists, turns, ups, and downs. Some who read this book may need to reread portions, and then prayerfully wait to hear from God to know if things I have stated are confirmed by Him. Why? Because not all you read, listen to, watch, or participate in is understood by others in the same way.

> **2 Timothy 2:15** states: "**Study** to shew thyself approved unto God, a workman that needeth not to be ashamed, **rightly dividing the word of truth.**"

Simply stated, when you study, you're showing God and others you're a person who is not ashamed of God, His Word, or the way of Salvation. This verse states and indicates that you should use your knowledge to place what you've read into perspective. That is how you are not ashamed. We need to study! Then, we need to ask for wisdom, knowledge, and understanding so we know the significance and importance of the Bible for ourselves. Even reading verses we have read before will bring about New Revelation for us. If you receive nothing else from studying His Word, rest assured, you will prove the most important fact of all: God is the One who makes no mistakes!

In closing this section, I say and state: "I believe every word that is found in the Holy Bible!"

There are times when I hear people claiming that they are speaking, teaching, or preaching God's Word. Though I may not agree with things they say or state, one thing I always do is pray the following short and direct prayer, and God always confirms or denies what they said. Try it for yourself:

"God, please do not allow me to receive a half–truth, for I want nothing but – "The Truth!" Please don't let me be deceived or tricked, for I want to know, live, and read "The Whole Truth." Amen!

5

Beginnings

CAUTION

Those with weak stomachs may not want to continue beyond this point. For the inquisitive and for those who have been seeking answers to their questions, this is one journey you will never forget!

Charges brought against the defendants are hideous, to say the least. Facts and evidence will show how these defendants, of their own accord, knowingly and willfully perpetrated acts and omissions in direct conflict with The Law in existence at the time of their crime. One remedy remains: a trial. The proceedings will adhere to the following format:

> Defendants will be heard by "The Judge"

> Evidence will be shown, documented, and recorded (in the Holy Bible), and

> The Judge will administer statutory and lawful justice. (Please note that your actions and omissions will be heard and considered before a decision is rendered at your trial as well.)

When the Bailiff reads the Indictment and Probable Cause, it will be the first time the defendants hear the charges that have been professed against them. This is a very sensitive case. Do not be surprised if we hear the judge declare total silence as this trial unfolds.

CRIMINAL INDICTMENT

INDICTMENT

<table>
<tr><td>State of Heaven
County of Love,</td><td align="right">SUPREME DISTRICT
#1 JUDICIAL DISTRICT
Court File #03
Prosecutor File #03</td></tr>
</table>

State of Heaven,
      Plaintiff,
VS.
ADAM
(Unknown – DOB), Summoned and Warranted
EVE
(Unknown – DOB), Summoned and Warranted
SERPENT
(Unknown – DOB), Summoned and Warranted

Defendants' address:
Garden of Eden
City of Paradise,
Earth – 000008
Order of Detention Issued
      Defendants,

The Complaint, being duly sworn, makes complaint to the above–named Court and states that there is probable cause to believe that the Defendants committed the offenses herein stated.

Each **COUNT** in this Indictment carries the same penalty, which is:

The **DEATH** Penalty

On or about the Eighth (8th) Day of Creation, Defendant 1, ADAM, Defendant 2, EVE, and Defendant 3, THE SERPENT, DID commit unlawful acts in opposition to the Law. Charges and allegations are as follows:

ALLEGED CHARGES AGAINST DEFENDANT 1 – ADAM

If Convicted, Each Count Warrants "The DEATH Penalty"

COUNT – I

ADAM committed known and willful acts, actions, and/or omissions in direct opposition to the Law, which are listed in the five (5) Counts against him. He knowingly participated in "Eating" **Forbidden Fruit** by his act, acts, actions, and/or omissions.

CHARGE:
Willing And Knowing Participation In "Eating Forbidden Fruit"

Heavenly Statute Violations:
Directive 1 and Directive 2

Maximum Sentence:
DEATH

COUNT – II

ADAM failed to protect the Garden of Eden from the demise of Defendant 3, THE SERPENT. His failure to protect "their" habitat/ home is a direct and blatant disregard **to act**, which is the Act of **Omission**.

CHARGE:
Failure To Perform Known AND Required Duties, or the Act of Omission

Heavenly Statute Violations:
Directive 1 and Directive 2

Maximum Sentence:
DEATH

COUNT – III

ADAM allowed communications between Defendant 2, EVE, and Defendant 3, THE SERPENT, resulting in a highly infectious and contagious disease being released from the Forbidden Fruit. His failure to act and/or to protect his helpmate in this situation shows his blatant refusal to comply with his duties and obligations. He was derelict in failing to appropriately intervene.

CHARGE:
Non–Intervention – OR – Dereliction of Duty

Heavenly Statute Violations:
Directive 1 and Directive 2

Maximum Sentence:
DEATH

COUNT – IV

ADAM failed to protect himself and his mate before she committed her criminal act(s). Eating/partaking of the forbidden fruit is considered a blatant "dereliction of duty."

CHARGE:
Failure to Protect "Eve" and himself, through dominion in the Garden of Eden

Heavenly Statute Violations:
Directive 1 and Directive 2

Maximum Sentence:
DEATH

COUNT – V

ADAM failed to impose and enforce his "Power of Dominion" in the Garden of Eden.

CHARGE:
Failure To Impose and Enforce his "Power of Dominion"

Heavenly Statute Violations:
Directive 1 and Directive 2

Maximum Sentence:
DEATH

CHARGES ALLEGED AGAINST DEFENDANT 2 – EVE

If Convicted, Each Count Warrants "The DEATH Penalty"

COUNT – I

EVE committed an unlawful act, which was "Eating" The Forbidden Fruit in direct opposition to The Law.

CHARGE:
Willing And Knowing Participation in Eating Forbidden Fruit

Heavenly Statute Violations:
Directive 1 and Directive 2

Maximum Sentence:
DEATH

COUNT – II

EVE committed an unlawful act, in direct opposition to the law, by allowing, without opposition, the Serpent to continue teasing and tempting her to eat the "Forbidden Fruit"

CHARGE:
Failure To Perform Known AND Required Duties, or the Act of Omission

Heavenly Statue Violations:
Directive 1 and Directive 2

Maximum Sentence:
DEATH

COUNT – III

EVE allowed acts to continually be committed in her presence, without informing her husband or telling THE SERPENT (unknown entity to her) to stop. This implied permission resulted in a highly infectious and contagious disease being released from the forbidden fruit, which infected EVE, ADAM, their eternal offspring, and the Garden of Eden, their perfectly created haven of continual tranquility and freedom from fear, freedom from discord, freedom from tension, freedom from sweating, freedom from hard manual labor, and more.

CHARGE:
Failure to Protect: Everything in the Garden of Eden.

Heavenly Statue Violations:
Directive 1 and Directive 2

Maximum Sentence:
DEATH

COUNT – IV

EVE committed an unlawful act, which was known to be in direct opposition to the Law. EVE failed to impose and enforce **"dominion,"** which was granted by **"The Law"**.

CHARGE:
Dereliction of Duty

Heavenly Statue Violations:
Directive 1 and Directive 2

Maximum Sentence:
DEATH

CHARGES ALLEGED AGAINST DEFENDANT 3 - THE SERPENT

If Convicted, Each Count Warrants "The DEATH Penalty"

COUNT – I

THE **SERPENT** willingly, knowingly, and with premeditation – through trickery – caused Defendant 1, ADAM, and Defendant 2, EVE, to eat **The Forbidden Fruit**, in direct opposition to **The Law**.

CHARGE:
Premeditated Murder

Heavenly Statute Violations:
Directive 1

Maximum Sentence:
DEATH

COUNT – II

THE **SERPENT** committed an unlawful act by knowingly masterminding the "Plot" to take over the world through Defendants 1 and 2. THE SERPENT failed to refrain from teaching, talking to, lying to, and/or coercing Defendant 1, ADAM, and Defendant 2, EVE.

CHARGE:
Coercion, Accomplice, Accessory, and a Knowing and Willing Participant

Heavenly Statute Violations:
Directives 1 and 2

Maximum Sentence:
DEATH

COUNT – III

THE **SERPENT** knew the acts and actions were in direct opposition
to the Law. His blatant and deliberate indifference in these criminal
acts shows his knowledgeable, intentional, and devious behavior,
which caused Defendant 1, ADAM, and Defendant 2, EVE, to eat
and/or partake of the forbidden fruit.

CHARGE:
Deliberate Indifference to Knowledgeable Reactions

Heavenly Statute Violations:
Directives 1 and 2

Maximum Sentence:
DEATH

COUNT – IV

THE **SERPENT** is charged with masterminding the offenses committed by Defendants 1 and 2. Should he be found guilty of any charge in this Indictment, he will qualify for Habitualization and the resulting enhanced penalties.

CHARGE:
Masterminding Criminal Acts committed by Defendants 1 and 2

Heavenly Statute Violations:
Directives 1 and 2

Maximum Sentence:
DEATH

STATEMENT OF PROBABLE CAUSE

STATEMENT OF PROBABLE CAUSE

The Complaint states that the following facts establish probable cause.

On or about the Eighth (8th) Day of Creation, ADAM and EVE, through individual and corporate means, committed unlawful acts and omissions, having violated known and clearly spoken Heavenly Statutes. With blatant disregard for the Law, these Defendants knew they were subjecting their lives and the lives of their offspring to a hideous, malicious, contagious infection that had no remedy or cure.

Each Defendant is charged separately and jointly as a willing party in criminal misconduct.

Defendant 1: **ADAM**, is charged with the following actions and/or omissions:

> ➤ Failure to enforce **"dominion over"** (subduing, protecting, and keeping) the Garden of Eden and its contents. Failure to **do his duty** violated two directives.

> ➤ He did not keep or try to prevent THE SERPENT from talking, teasing, coercing, and lying to EVE. Eventually, after much teasing, coercing, etc., Eve touched, picked, held, and/or ate The Forbidden Fruit from The Forbidden Tree, which caused an incurable infection. Knowingly doing this violated the directives and commandments, which were spoken, known, and understood by ADAM.

> ➤ Of his own accord, ADAM also accepted from Eve the known to be "Forbidden Fruit" and ate of it, as EVE did, which he knew was in direct contradiction to the Law.

Defendant 2: **EVE**, is charged with the following acts, actions, and/ or omissions:

> ➤ Refusal to adhere to the directives and warnings of her husband, ADAM, to enforce dominion over everything in the Garden of Eden, especially over THE SERPENT, who coerced and enticed EVE to do things contrary to the Law.

> ➤ EVE chose not to help in protecting their lives, being insubordinate in her actions, which resulted in a worldwide spread of an infectious disease.

> ➤ EVE did touch, take part in, hold onto, and partake of the Forbidden Fruit in opposition to the Law.

> ➤ EVE, knowing she had done wrong, also offered ADAM what both knew to be forbidden, "The Fruit," thereby causing him to be a willing and knowing participant and to be infected with the same malicious and incurable disease. This act, while not premeditated, was in opposition to the Law.

Defendant 3: **SERPENT**, is charged with the following accusations and allegations:

a. Being an accessory to the acts, actions, and/or omissions of ADAM and EVE.

b. Masterminding the actions that occurred in the Garden of Eden.

c. Intentionally using unscrupulous means against Defendants 1 and 2, which caused their actions and omissions to be fruitful.

d. SERPENT is a formerly charged, tried, and convicted criminal. It is necessary to "**<u>Habitualize</u>**" THE SERPENT for his actions in accordance with the Law.

COMPLAINT

REQUEST

Complainant requests that these Defendants, subject to bail or conditions of release, be:

a. Arrested, or that other lawful steps be taken to obtain Defendants' appearance in court; or

b. Detained, if already in custody, pending further proceedings, and that said Defendants otherwise be dealt with according to the Law.

COMPLAINANT'S NAME: **GOD**

COMPLAINANT'S SIGNATURE: *God*

Subscribed and sworn to before the undersigned
this 08th day of Creation, 0000.

NAME/TITLE: SIGNATURE:

GOD ALMIGHTY   *God Almighty*

Being authorized to prosecute the offenses charged,
I approve this complaint.

Date: 01/08/0000

Prosecuting Attorney's Signature:
Son of God

Registration Number: 1

FINDING OF PROBABLE CAUSE

From the above–sworn facts, and any supporting affidavits or supplemental sworn testimony, I, the Issuing Officer, have determined that probable cause exists to support, subject to bail or conditions of release where applicable, Defendants' arrest, or otherwise Lawful steps to be taken, to obtain Defendants' appearance in court, or Defendants' detention, if already in custody, pending further proceedings. These Defendants are therefore charged with the above–stated offense/s.

[X] SUMMONS

THEREFORE YOU, THE ABOVE–NAMED DEFENDANTS, ARE HEREBY SUMMONED to appear on the (8th) Eighth day of Creation, at Noon before the above–named Court at The Supreme Court of Courts, In Heaven and Above Earth, to answer this complaint.

IF YOU FAIL TO APPEAR in response to this SUMMONS, a WARRANT FOR YOUR ARREST shall be issued.

[X] WARRANT

To the Sheriff of the above–named county, or the person authorized to execute this warrant: I hereby order, in the name of the State of Heaven, that the above–name Defendants be apprehended and arrested without delay and brought promptly before the above–named Court (if in session), and if not, before a Judge or Judicial Officer of such Court without unnecessary delay, and in any event not later than thirty–six (36) hours after the arrest or as soon as such Judge or Judicial Officer is available to be dealt with according to the Law.

[X] Execute on Earth Only

[X] Execute Worldwide

[X] Execute in Garden of Eden

[X] ORDER OF DETENTION

Since the above–named Defendants are already in custody, I hereby order, subject to bail or conditions of release, that the above–named Defendants continue to be detained pending further proceedings.

The above–named Defendants are not to be released for any reason prior to their trial.

Bail:
NONE

Conditions of Release:
NOT TO BE RELEASED

This complaint, duly subscribed and sworn to, is issued by the undersigned Judicial Officer this 08ᵗʰ day of Creation.

JUDICIAL OFFICER:	**GOD**
SIGNATURE:	*God*
NAME:	**PROSECUTOR**
TITLE:	**PROSECUTOR**

Sworn testimony has been given before the Judicial Officer by the following witness: **GOD**

COUNTY OF LOVE, STATE OF HEAVEN

STATE OF HEAVEN,

Plaintiff,

vs.

Adam. Eve. Serpent,

Defendants,

Clerk's Signature or File Stamp:

FILED 01/08/0000

RETURN OF SERVICE
I hereby Certify and Return that I have served a
copy of this SUMMONS and WARRANT upon
the Defendants herein named.

Signature of Authorized Service Agent:
Michael - Archangel

ATTACHMENT **A**

DEFENDANT NAME:
Adam (the first man to be hand–formed)

Defendant Alias Name(s):   N/A

Defendant DOB: 00-05-0000

Alias DOB: N/A

Defendant Last Known Address:
Garden of Eden, Paradise, Earth

State ID:
Adam - only hand–formed man

DEFENDANT NAME:
Eve (first hand–formed woman)

Defendant Alias Name(s): N/A

Defendant DOB: 00-07-0000

Alias DOB: N/A

Defendant Last Known Address:
Garden of Eden, Paradise, Earth

State ID:
Eve - first hand–first woman

DEFENDANT NAME:
Serpent

Defendant Alias Name(s):
Lucifer, Satan, Father of Lies, the Evil One, Your Adversary, the Devil, etc...

Defendant DOB: 00-00-0000

Alzas DOB: N/A

Defendant Last Known Address:
Garden of Eden, Paradise, Earth

State ID:
Serpent - evil, disguised as good.

The Defendants have now
entered the courtroom

This case has a Prosecutor

Defendants chose to
represent themselves

They are claiming innocence

It is time for the trial to begin

**In and Before the
Supreme Court of Courts
In Heaven And On Earth**

Heavenly Prosecutor
Prosecutor,

VS.

**ADAM, EVE, and
SERPENT,
Defendants,**

CASE 00003

**ACTS AND/OR OMISSIONS AGAINST
THE DIVINELY SPOKEN WORDS OF GOD**

---

1   BAILIFF: Everyone, please rise as the Honorable
2   Judge enters and is seated. The Honorable and
3   Holy Judge of ALL, God Almighty, presides today.
4
5
6   The case before this Honorable Court is held in
7   accordance with The Law. Due to the serious
8   consequences this tragic incident will have on
9   those living now and for generations to follow, this
10   case must be heard and a decision rendered today.
11
12
13   Once this trial begins, you are expected to remain
14   seated and quiet, so all parties have an opportunity
15   to be heard.
16
17
18   The Judge, dressed in a white robe, enters the
19   courtroom. He is smiling and nodding. He walks
20   boldly and with great authority to the bench,
21   surveys the courtroom and slowly sits.
22
23
24   It is so quiet that a leaf could begin its descent to
25   the ground and be heard.
26
27
28   **BAILIFF**: Everyone may now be seated.
29
30
31   **JUDGE**: Bailiff, you may proceed with opening

1   remarks.

2

3

4   **Naming of First Defendant**

5

6

7   **BAILIFF:** Your Honor, the first Defendant to be

8   named is ADAM, husband of EVE, the first

9   "hand–formed" man, and father of future

10   generations. By Divine appointment and

11   designation, ADAM was the ruler and caretaker

12   of the Garden of Eden, where the alleged criminal

13   acts, actions, and omissions took place.

14

15

16   **Naming of Second Defendant**

17

18

19   **BAILIFF:** The second Defendant, EVE, is none

20   other than the wife of ADAM, the mother of future

21   generations. EVE was hand–formed specifically,

22   to be a helpmate for Defendant 1, ADAM

23

24

25   **Naming of Third Defendant**

26

27

28   **BAILIFF:** Unbeknownst to Defendants 1 and 2,

29   the third Defendant is more than an accomplice.

30   This defendant is a former heavenly angel. His

31   previous criminal actions will have no bearing on

1   the case being tried today.

2

3

4   However, because of the sentence imposed in that
5   trial, he was confined to Earth. While here, he
6   took on the bodily form of a reptile. Defendant 1,
7   ADAM, had cause to name him, through the
8   power of dominion, which Adam used in naming
9   Defendant 3, "SERPENT."

10

11

12   These Defendants are charged with criminal
13   misconduct by their individual acts, actions, and
14   omissions against the Law. They were
15   well–informed.

16

17

18   Their alleged crimes are as follows:

19

20   a) Willingly and knowingly touching, taking, and
21   eating Forbidden Fruit;

22

23   b) Intentionally and deliberately engaging in
24   improprieties;

25

26   c) Failing to use Dominion and follow spoken and
27   understood Directives;

28

29   d) Independently and Corporately violating
30   Heavenly Statutes (Directives 1 and 2)

31

1   Only Defendant 3 is charged and tried today as
2   a **Habitual** Offender
3
4
5   All parties intelligently, willingly, knowingly, and
6   with blatant and willful disregard for their own
7   safety and welfare, intentionally disobeyed the
8   spoken directives (also known as
9   commandments), which clearly stated,
10
11   "…thou shalt not eat of it…"[1]
12   (the Forbidden Tree and Fruit).
13
14
15   These commandments were given to ADAM and
16   understood by him.
17
18
19   ADAM then disclosed these instructions to EVE.[2]
20   She knew the ramifications and penalties for
21   partaking of the Tree of Knowledge of Good and
22   Evil and its Fruit.
23
24
25   These two Defendants (pointing again at ADAM
26   and EVE), as well as all their offspring, were
27   created to be and intended to remain in perfect
28   condition.
29
30
31   Their intentional disobedience caused the evil

1   contained within this tree and its fruit to be
2   dispersed, infecting not only their nature, but that
3   of all mankind.
4
5
6   Many innocent people, including children, will
7   replenish the Earth and continue to pay the
8   penalty for these alleged crimes committed by
9   ADAM, EVE, and SERPENT.
10
11
12   (The Bailiff points at the Defendants and
13   continues speaking.)
14
15
16   **BAILIFF:** The Law in effect at the time of their
17   alleged criminal behavior must be used in this
18   trial.
19
20
21   That same law will assist in rendering a just
22   decision. It is by this law – spoken, known, and
23   understood by these Defendants – that they must
24   be tried. Penalties, should there be any, will come
25   because of a determination of innocence or guilt.
26
27
28   The Law clearly declares the penalty upon the
29   determination of guilt, and that penalty is
30   DEATH!
31

1   This is the only Court with jurisdiction to hear
2   this case and render a decision.
3
4
5   (Wiping the sweat from his brow, he continues.)
6
7
8   **BAILIFF:** The duty of this Court is to ask each
9   Defendant how he or she pleads to the charges
10   presented.
11
12
13   ADAM, what is your answer to these allegations?
14
15
16   Are you innocent or guilty as charged?
17
18
19   (ADAM looks at the other Defendants, especially
20   his wife, EVE. He doesn't want to be trapped by
21   his own words, so he takes a moment.)
22
23
24   **ADAM:** Not Guilty!
25
26
27   The Judge looks at ADAM and the charges against
28   him, and then nods for the Bailiff to go on.
29
30
31   **BAILIFF:** How say thee, EVE? Are you innocent

1   or guilty of the charges against you?
2
3
4   (EVE, stunned by ADAM's response, stands
5   proudly and answers like ADAM.)
6
7
8   **EVE:** Not Guilty!
9
10
11   EVE sits down but continues to look at ADAM
12   quizzically.
13
14
15   The judge looks at EVE and then nods once
16   again, allowing the Bailiff to proceed.
17
18
19   **BAILIFF:** How say thee, SERPENT, are you
20   innocent or guilty of these charges?
21
22
23   The SERPENT remains seated, smiles, and nods
24   at the Bailiff but offers no response. He looks at
25   ADAM and EVE, the Judge, and then, still
26   smirking, sits back comfortably, knowing, so he
27   thinks, the outcome.
28
29
30   The Judge leans forward, arms on the desktop,
31   and speaks in an agitated and unquestionably

1   loud and authoritative voice. The look on his
2   face is frightening. The Judge repeats,
3   "How Say Thee, Serpent?"
4
5
6   **JUDGE:** SERPENT, are you mocking this court?
7   Perhaps you mock these proceedings? It doesn't
8   matter if you answer or not, I am going to render
9   a verdict today on your actions and the actions
10 of the other Defendants.
11
12
13 However, due to your insubordination in this
14 courtroom and toward these proceedings, your
15 punishment should you be found guilty, will be
16 enforced PERMANENTLY![3]
17
18
19 Bailiff, pardon my interruption, but my
20 courtroom will not be mocked by this
21 Defendant or by anyone else!
22
23
24 (With more calm, He says) You may proceed.
25
26
27 **BAILIFF:** Your Honor, I have read the charges
28 against these Defendants.
29
30
31 Defendants 1 and 2 claim innocence. The Court

1   has heard and recorded their pleas of
2   "Not Guilty."
3
4
5   Defendant 3, the Serpent, neither admits nor
6   denies innocence or guilt. A plea of
7   "Nolo Contendere" is entered on his behalf.
8   The reading of charges and the entering of
9   pleas have been completed. I turn these
10   proceedings over to you, Sir.
11
12
13   **JUDGE:** Ladies and gentlemen, the case before
14   the Court today is astounding in many ways.
15   You will hear things that surpass what you can
16   imagine. It is the right, duty, and obligation of
17   this Court to hear testimony from both sides
18   before I render a decision.
19
20
21   The Prosecution makes many accusations.
22   Evidence will be presented to demonstrate that
23   each of the defendants committed the criminal
24   acts, actions, and/or omissions with which they
25   are charged. I warn you to maintain your silence
26   during this important and highly sensitive case.
27
28
29   This Court has the right, duty, and obligation to
30   conduct this criminal trial. It holds jurisdiction
31   based on the location of these criminal activities.

1   This trial is warranted in order to prove or
2   disprove the alleged acts, actions, and/or
3   omissions of these Defendants.
4
5
6   If the accusations are found to be true, this trial
7   will continue, and a verdict will be rendered
8   and enforced today!
9
10
11   Bailiff, have the Defendants been sworn in?
12
13
14   **BAILIFF:** Yes, your Honor, the Defendants
15   have been sworn in.
16
17
18   **JUDGE:** The Prosecution may proceed with
19   opening statements
20
21
22   **PROSECUTOR**: (stands)
23
24
25   Thank you, Your Honor. If it pleases the Court,
26   I want to start with the alleged charges against
27   these Defendants. I plan to introduce evidence
28   that will prove that the allegations made in this
29   case are not only warrant this trial, but also
30   warrant an immediate decision.
31

1   I believe the evidence I present will leave these

2   Defendants defenseless. I believe they thought

3   the evidence had been lost or hidden and was

4   irretrievable; however, the evidence will prove

5   the allegations made in this case are not only

6   truthful, but justifiable.

7

8

9   **JUDGE:** If what you state is true, a decision by

10   this court will be swift and justified. Continue

11   please.

12

13

14   **PROSECUTOR:** This is a very serious case;

15   the Defendants are accused of horrendous

16   criminal misconduct.

17

18

19   Each Defendant claims to have acted

20   independently of the other, but I will prove

21   that their actions and lack of actions necessitates

22   both individual and corporate punishment for

23   compliance and participation with one another.

24

25

26   The Defendants (pointing) knew the directives

27   that were issued to them, yet they chose to do

28   what they desired. That is the reason we are

29   here today.

30

31

1 These defendants are guilty as charged! Let the
2 records reflect this case against a husband and
3 wife, who will forever be known as ADAM
4 and EVE.
5
6
7 Finally, Your Honor, there is the matter of the
8 SERPENT.
9
10
11 One of the criminal acts (pointing at the
12 SERPENT) Defendant 3 committed is different
13 from those committed by Defendants 1 and 2.
14
15
16 It's mentioned due to its significance. The effect
17 of these crimes, which are now embedded within
18 ADAM and EVE will enter all future humans
19 through conception and birth. It will be called
20 love. The love I speak of is the evil desire or
21 lust for things that are not to be known, explored,
22 touched, or tasted.
23
24
25 This type of love is deadly and contagious. It has
26 created the ability to know how to lie.
27
28
29 I said all I need to say at this time, Your Honor.
30
31

1   The BAILIFF rises and speaks to the audience.
2
3
4   **BAILIFF:** For now, these Defendants are
5   merely accused. They have not been found
6   guilty of any criminal misconduct,
7   individually or corporately.
8
9
10   As you sit and listen, consider for yourself
11   whether the accusations, allegations, and
12   arguments made are true and just. You are not a
13   jury with a job; you are not "fact finders."
14
15
16   Your opinions will not help render a decision in
17   this case.
18
19
20   This court is obligated to render fair and
21   impartial rulings and, if necessary, to pronounce
22   an appropriate punishment.
23
24
25   JUDGE: Ladies and gentlemen, this is a very
26   serious criminal case. Lives are at stake.
27   Both sides will be allowed to present their
28   accusations, answers, and evidence.
29
30
31   In rendering an accurate verdict, I must use the

1   law in existence at the time of the criminal acts
2   and/or omissions of those named.
3
4
5   Prosecutor, you may proceed with your case
6   and opening statements.
7
8
9   **PROSECUTOR**: Thank you, Your Honor.
10   As I begin the prosecution against the
11   Defendants, I want to reiterate that ADAM
12   and EVE are charged with criminal misconduct
13
14
15   But I will prove, beyond any reasonable doubt
16   that they are highly contagious with a disease
17   that is called sin.
18
19
20   It is the recommendation of the Prosecution that
21   ADAM and EVE must be banned forever from
22   ALL the trees in the Garden of Eden.
23
24
25   Their disease came from the Forbidden Fruit
26   that was on the Tree of Knowledge of Good
27   and Evil. That tree and the Tree of Life still
28   stand in the middle of the Garden.
29
30
31

1   These trees must be off limits to the Defendants
2   forever.
3
4
5   The Forbidden Fruit gave them forbidden
6   knowledge. The fruit itself housed forbidden
7   elements. This fruit was forbidden to them
8   from the onset, and they knew it
9
10
11   Therefore, it has caused the greatest infestation
12   ever. It is none other than sin!
13
14
15   Presently, this disease is incurable. It is the first
16   cause of death, as well as being one of the
17   punishments required for their acts and
18   omissions against the warnings or directives
19   known to them.
20
21
22   Each defendant has been formally charged.
23
24   Their claims are:
25
26   **a**. Neither is responsible nor liable for acts,
27   actions, and/or omissions of the other;
28
29   **b**. Each is independent of the other;
30
31   **c**. Neither should be charged or punished for

1   corporate punishments; and

2

3   **d**. Each should be considered innocent of their
4   current charges.

5

6

7   Each Defendant is charged with individual
8   and corporate criminal misconduct. Accusations
9   have been made against Defendants 1 and 2,
10   ADAM and EVE, individually and corporately,
11   but they claim these charges are faulty.

12

13

14   The charges read into the records before this
15   honorable Court are factually correct!

16

17

18   ADAM and EVE also claim that their actions
19   and omissions are the result of a third party
20   and their individual charges should be dropped
21   and dismissed.

22

23

24   The evidence I presented requires justice to be
25   administered immediately and in accordance with
26   the Law.

27

28

29   The magnitude of this case goes beyond simple
30   disobedience. We must also consider those who
31   have not been named in this trial, but who will

1   be infected with the disease of sin by virtue of
2   their birth.
3
4
5   Future children will be forced to suffer for a
6   crime they did not personally commit.
7
8
9   (Looking disdainfully at Defendant 3, the
10   Prosecutor continues.
11
12
13   THE SERPENT, also known as Satan,
14   the Enemy, the Evil One, and the Father of
15   Lies, is also charged individually and
16   corporately for his active and intentional
17   participation in this criminal misconduct.
18
19
20   My recommendation for these intentional
21   criminal acts and omissions requires one
22   punishment, the Death Sentence.
23
24
25   This penalty is not too harsh; they knew the
26   consequences before they ate from the forbidden
27   Tree of Knowledge of Good and Evil.
28
29
30   This (turning to display a piece of fruit to the
31   spectators in the Courtroom) is the Forbidden

1   Fruit that ADAM and EVE did not finish.
2
3
4   I submit this evidence as Prosecutor's Exhibit 1.
5
6
7   As you can see, it has not been completely
8   consumed.
9
10
11   This fruit is from the only forbidden tree in the
12   Garden of Eden, the Tree of Knowledge of
13   Good and Evil.
14
15
16   Defendant 2, EVE, desired this fruit. She
17   intentionally chose to touch, hold, and partake
18   of it. And then, she turned to the man who
19   stood beside her, Defendant 1, ADAM, and
20   handed him the forbidden fruit, of which he
21   willingly partook as Eve had done.
22
23
24   These Defendants, whether individual or
25   corporate, are guilty of the charges brought
26   against them today.
27
28
29   The obvious marks in and on this piece of fruit
30   prove, beyond any reasonable doubt, this fruit
31   has been touched, picked, tasted, and was eaten.

1   This evidence plainly shows willful and
2   intentional disobedience by ADAM and EVE.
3   Nothing other than what the Law proffers as
4   the penalty would be appropriate. I state again,
5   the Law says they deserve death!
6
7
8   I have no other evidence to produce at this time,
9   Your Honor.
10
11
12   (The JUDGE now focuses His attention on
13   the Defendants, fixing them with a brief stare.)
14
15
16   **JUDGE:** ADAM, is this the truth?
17
18   Have you done what the Prosecutor has accused
19   you of doing? Have you gone so far as to touch,
20   hold, and eat the Forbidden Fruit?
21
22   Were you forced to do this?
23
24   Were you tricked into committing this
25   unforgivable act?
26
27   Are you part of this corporate crime?
28
29   If you were not in any shape, form, or fashion
30   involved in this, I need you to say so. ADAM,
31   are you guilty?

1   (ADAM hangs his head in shame.)

2

3   **JUDGE:** And now, EVE, I ask you the same

4   questions.

5

6   Are the allegations truthful?

7

8   Have you done what the Prosecutor has

9   accused you of doing?

10

11   Have you gone so far as to touch, hold,

12   partake of this known to be forbidden fruit?

13

14   And then you handed your husband, ADAM, the

15   Forbidden Fruit?

16

17   Were you tricked into committing this

18   unpardonable act?

19

20   Were you coerced, EVE? If you, in any way,

21   shape, form, or fashion, are involved in this

22   crime, I need you to say so. Are you guilty?

23

24   Well, are you two going to answer?

25

26   (EVE now follows ADAM's lead and

27   shamefully hangs her head as well.)

28

29   **JUDGE:** Do either of you want to say something

30   in your defense? Do you want to counter these

31   serious accusations?

1   **JUDGE:** ADAM, you knew the directives that
2   were issued: never were you to partake of
3   anything from the forbidden tree
4   The Prosecutor alleges you willingly disobeyed,
5   and the Law stipulates the penalty for
6   noncompliance.
7
8
9   (GOD pauses for a moment, pondering what He
10   can, within legal boundaries, do in regards to the
11   consequences. Suddenly, He smiles, lifts His
12   head, and continues.)
13
14
15   **JUDGE:** The rules mentioned to you, and
16   which you were to convey to EVE, before the
17   two of you deliberately decided to disobey was
18   given as a warning, and the consequences were
19   spoken, right?
20
21
22   One thing that comes to mind may be worth
23   looking into, but at this time we will continue
24   with these proceedings. OK!
25
26
27   You three have heard the charges, and you have
28   seen what the Prosecutor has presented as
29   evidence. According to the Prosecutor, this
30   evidence came from the forbidden tree. This is
31   your opportunity to defend yourself.

1 ADAM, I am giving you the first opportunity
2 to speak, and if possible, justify what you did
3 or did not do corporately and independently.
4
5
6 It has been said that you totally disregarded
7 the directives that were issued as a warning
8 for your protection. Do you have anything to
9 say in your defense? Speak now or forever
10 hold your peace!
11
12
13 **ADAM:** Thank you, Your Honor. I tried. I really
14 tried to stay away from that tree. It was the
15 woman YOU (accusingly) made and gave to me…
16
17
18 **JUDGE:** Are you accusing Me of being an
19 accomplice? Am I guilty because I made Eve to
20 ease your loneliness? Are you sure you want to
21 accuse Me? Tell Me why you are so quick to
22 accuse ME.
23
24
25 **ADAM:** (Crying, his voice fearfully loud.) NO,
26 NO, NO, Your Honor. I didn't mean it that way.
27 I wasn't accusing You. I was merely trying to
28 point out that You made and Gave me (staring
29 defiantly at EVE) **that woman.** If not for "that
30 woman," the one who was created for me, the
31 one who offered me (clearly agitated) that fruit,

1   I wouldn't be charged with any improprieties,
2   and I wouldn't be on trial today.
3
4
5   What I'm trying to say is, she tempted me
6   with the fruit. I never would have touched or
7   eaten it, but she wouldn't stop teasing and
8   tempting me.
9
10
11   If she had never gone to the tree and admired
12   the fruit like she did, touching it so tenderly,
13   with such deep, passionate longing, sensuously
14   caressing it, I wouldn't be on trial, and I
15   wouldn't be in trouble for actions I didn't
16   commit.
17
18
19   If any one of you heard the sounds I did when
20   she tasted the fruit and saw the desire in her eyes
21   for the fruit, I wouldn't be on trial for her
22   deliberate insubordination. Your Honor,
23
24
25   (shaking his head in disbelief)
26
27
28   I could not stop her.
29
30
31   EVE is the one who touched, picked, held, and

1   tasted that fruit first! She accepted the things …
2
3
4   (pointing at the SERPENT)
5
6
7   …he told her. Therefore, it's because of her that
8   I was tricked into tasting the fruit.
9
10
11   The way she tempted me was something I had
12   never felt before. She definitely deserves to be
13   punished. I, on the other hand, should be set
14   free. The charges against me should be
15   dropped.
16
17
18   I admit that I accepted the fruit, but I repeat sir,
19   it was all her fault! She needs to pay the penalty
20   for what she did to me and to our children. It
21   was nothing more than curiosity on my part.
22
23
24   I wanted to see what would happen after she
25   touched and ate the forbidden fruit. If she had
26   never been made and given to me, I wouldn't
27   be on trial, and there would be no charges
28   against me.
29
30
31   (The JUDGE leans forward angrily.)

1   **JUDGE:** ADAM, am I hearing you correctly?
2
3

4   Are you accusing Me again? How, exactly, did I
5   participate in your criminal misconduct? If you
6   had protected EVE, as you were supposed to do,
7   instead of watching while she touched and ate
8   the Forbidden Fruit, then I wouldn't be hearing
9   this case or your petty plea for leniency. Neither
10   would I hear your indirect accusations
11   concerning Me.
12
13

14   You and your mate, ADAM, are the reason we
15   are having this trial!
16
17   Do you have more to say?
18
19

20   **ADAM:** Please forgive me, Your Honor, but I
21   didn't mean to be accusing You of anything,
22   except for one fact, Sir – You created her, and
23   You openly admit this.
24
25   If that woman had not been given to me, I would
26   not be charged with any criminal misconduct. I
27   should be pardoned and all allegations against
28   me should be dismissed.
29
30   It was her trickery that caused me to hide.
31   I believe once you hear the whole story, You

1   will find me innocent.

2

3   Definitively and unequivocally, EVE is guilty

4   and I am not.

5

6   (ADAM now points toward EVE and the

7   SERPENT.)

8

9   **ADAM:** They worked together! The fact is the

10   SERPENT and EVE are guilty!

11

12   They need to be convicted and punished for

13   their cunning and deceiving ways, not me.

14

15

16   (The Judge bangs His gavel repeatedly, trying to

17   get ADAM's attention.)

18

19

20   **JUDGE:** Now, EVE, it is your turn to defend

21   yourself against the Prosecutor's accusations.

22   Additionally, I want to hear your response to

23   what ADAM has said. What do you have to say

24   in your defense, EVE?

25

26

27   **EVE:** It's not fair for you to pardon ADAM and

28   not pardon me! Everything that took place in the

29   Garden of Eden, I mean the things that we are

30   charged with, was due to the SERPENT's

31   confusing and cunning words. The whole thing

1   was his idea, not mine.
2
3

4   Sir, there is the one who deceitfully used my
5   curiosity and convinced me to consider the
6   Forbidden Fruit.
7

8   He twisted words, and they sounded correct.
9   I didn't know what to do.
10

11   (EVE tearfully points her finger at the
12   SERPENT.)
13
14

15   **EVE:** He is completely at fault! He kept taking
16   fruit from the forbidden tree. He kept doing it
17   in front of me. He made sounds I never heard
18   before, and they appealed to me. I watched him
19   closely, but he never seemed to change. I'm
20   talking about this dying thing. And then, I
21   wondered if ADAM told me the truth.
22

23   ADAM said we would die if we ate the
24   Forbidden Fruit, but I didn't see THE
25   SERPENT die.
26

27   What was I to believe?
28

29   So, out of curiosity more than anything else, I
30   started to believe what the SERPENT said. Yes,
31   I admit that I partook of the Forbidden Fruit, but

1   honestly, it seemed harmless.
2
3
4   The tree was pleasant to look at, and the fruit
5   the Serpent took from the tree was so pretty.
6   I thought the SERPENT was right. He didn't
7   die or change in a way that was noticeable
8   when he touched, held, and accepted the fruit
9   that was supposed to cause death.
10
11   (Eve shakes her head.)
12
13   Maybe I made a mistake, but when the
14   SERPENT touched, held, and talked to me
15   about how the fruit was so enjoyable, I
16   finally decided to try some for myself.
17   Adam was with me, and he didn't try to
18   stop me. I questioned Adam's honesty.
19
20   The fruit seemed to make the most
21   enjoyable and enticing sounds while the
22   Serpent was eating it. I wondered who was
23   telling me the truth: Was it ADAM or the
24   SERPENT?
25
26   YOU never told me not to eat the fruit from
27   the forbidden tree. It was always ADAM
28   who ordered me around, so it seemed, and he
29   was always telling me what I could and could
30   not do in the Garden...
31

1 **JUDGE:** Are you, like ADAM, accusing
2 ME of having a part in your criminal
3 misconduct, Eve? I do not even have to
4 hear any more to render a decision, but I am
5 fair and just and I am giving you a chance
6 to defend your actions and inactions, Eve.
7
8
9 Would you like to proceed with your defense
10 or are you going to continue to accuse me,
11 as Adam did?
12
13
14 **EVE:** Your Honor, I apologize for anything
15 that sounded like I was accusing You. I
16 want to continue, Sir.
17
18
19 When I ate the fruit, I did not die. In fact, I
20 had no idea what dying was. So, what was I
21 to think except that, ADAM, lied or made a
22 mistake by keeping the truth from me
23 concerning the tree of knowledge of good
24 and evil?
25
26
27 Once I saw with my own eyes how the
28 SERPENT ate the fruit, and nothing
29 happened to him, I gently grazed the fruit
30 with my fingertips. Eventually, I was brave
31 enough to taste it, but ADAM stood beside

1   me and did not say anything. ADAM was
2   the one You appointed to be in charge; I
3   certainly didn't know any better. Was I not
4   taken from under his arm to be protected
5   by him?
6
7
8   (Eve takes a brief pause, and then says)
9
10
11   ADAM took and willingly ate the forbidden
12   fruit, too!
13
14
15   **JUDGE:** Eve! Are you saying that it is the
16   SERPENT who is the guilty party here and
17   not you?
18
19
20   Or am I to believe that you are saying it is
21   all ADAM's fault? Are you trying to
22   convince Me that you are innocent? Your
23   own confession sentences you!
24
25
26   (Scornfully) You don't have the authority to
27   judge others and yet you attempt to assign
28   blame to clear yourself. I AM the Only One
29   Who has the right and power to judge.
30
31

1   (Eve boldly interrupts)
2
3
4   **EVE:** I deserve a pardon if ADAM receives
5   one!
6
7
8   ADAM was responsible for me; YOU gave
9   him charge over everything in the Garden of
10   Eden.
11
12
13   Eating the Forbidden fruit was the
14   SERPENT's idea from the very beginning.
15   He told me to touch it. I even told the
16   SERPENT that ADAM and I were not
17   allowed to eat anything from that tree, but
18   he laughed. He confused me with his words
19   and questions. For the record, Your Honor, I
20   never forced or tried to force ADAM to eat
21   the fruit! He willingly stood right there
22   beside me.
23
24
25   Adam didn't do anything to try to stop me,
26   even though he had the right, duty, power,
27   and an obligation to do so! ADAM took the
28   forbidden fruit I offered to him, and he ate
29   it, just like I did. If he gets a pardon, so do I,
30   if this is a fair and impartial trial!
31

1   **JUDGE:** Put your hand down, ADAM!
2   Your opportunity to refute EVE's
3   statements will come later!
4
5
6   Now then, SERPENT, it is time for your
7   explanation for your apparent and active
8   role in this serious matter before this court.
9
10
11   Make it a good one. I remind you that you
12   lost your previous case in this courtroom.
13   Maybe this time you will not lie – or is that
14   too much to ask of you?
15
16
17   **SERPENT:** Those two are guilty as you
18   stated earlier, with one obvious exception,
19   I am not guilty of forcing either one to do
20   what You forbade. I did talk to EVE, but I
21   also spoke to ADAM long before I ever
22   spoke to her. ADAM saw me eat the fruit,
23   just like EVE, yet he did not try to stop me
24   from eating the (forbidden to them) fruit
25   or tell me to stop talking to EVE.
26
27
28   She decided by herself to touch and try the
29   fruit they both knew to be forbidden to them.
30
31

1   EVE acknowledged that ADAM had told
2   her about the Forbidden Fruit on the Tree
3   of Knowledge of Good and Evil.
4
5
6   She told me so, but still she did what she wanted. I
7   never forced either one to do anything they did not
8   want to do long before I spoke to them.
9   ADAM is no less guilty than the woman he
10   named EVE. He observed her desire and
11   considered the same fruit before Eve ever
12   got up the courage to touch it, take it, hold
13   it, and eat it, and he never tried to stop her.
14   Yes, I spoke to them, but I am not guilty of
15   any crime or criminal act, unless You claim
16   that speaking to them is a criminal offense?
17   I did not hypnotize them or force them to
18   touch or eat from the Tree! They made those
19   choices out of their own free will.
20
21
22   (Pointing at God) YOU are the One who
23   placed free will in them, which is why they
24   chose to partake of the forbidden fruit!
25
26
27   **JUDGE:** (Angrily states) SERPENT, I
28   cannot believe you, like Adam and EVE, are
29   accusing ME of being an accomplice in these
30   criminal acts. I remind you that you have
31   already been condemned once to a death

1   sentence, which you are currently serving.
2   Now you are in jeopardy that I will add to
3   Your punishment for your blatant disregard
4   for the beings I made with My own hands
5   and placed in the Garden of Eden to live
6   forever.
7
8
9   I will still allow you to finish your speech,
10   then judgment will be delivered.
11
12
13   **SERPENT:** I say it again: I am totally
14   innocent of their willful wrongdoings.
15   Why should I be punished for their willful
16   and deliberate criminal acts?
17
18
19   I never forced them into anything! If I had,
20   I would be the one who has Authority and
21   power to rule and make decisions in the
22   Garden of Eden, but it's ADAM who has
23   that power, not me. I could never say
24   anything to change Your mind, so my speech is…
25
26
27   (laughingly saying)
28
29   "fruitless."
30
31

1   (The Judge looks straight forward,
2   unamused, and now showing signs of being
3   tired of the arrogant defendants in front of
4   Him.)
5
6
7   **SERPENT:** I have nothing else to say!
8   There is nothing I can say that You don't
9   already know. I do, however, ask for mercy
10   concerning this situation and these charges.
11
12
13   **JUDGE:** Prosecutor, do you have anything
14   further You would like to say?
15
16
17   (The Prosecutor stands, shakes His head no
18   as He has nothing to add, but as He starts to
19   sit down, He resumes.)
20
21
22   **PROSECUTOR:** No, Your Honor. What
23   more can I say when the Defendants
24   admitted, through their own testimony,
25   about their willful and active participation in
26   the criminal charges?
27
28
29   **JUDGE:** Well then, if all sides have been
30   heard, I'll render My Decision and pass
31   judgment as required…

1   (Judge pauses for a moment, sits back in His
2   Chair, looks at the evidence, and then says)
3
4
5   **THE LAW** was and is specific concerning
6   the consequences for acts and omissions
7   contrary to the Heavenly Statutes.
8
9
10   There is only ONE penalty according to
11   **THE LAW**, and the only remedy is death!
12   And yet, You, Prosecutor, contemplate
13   leniency? Sir, I invite You to reconsider.
14
15
16   (ADAM, EVE, and THE SERPENT raise
17   their hands quickly trying to interrupt the
18   Judge.)
19
20
21   **JUDGE:** I recognize Your concern,
22   Counselor, but I know what's best. as
23   Adjudicator. I must deliver a fair verdict for
24   each Defendant.
25
26
27   (Noticing the wildly waving arms of the
28   Defendants)
29
30
31   I also see that the three named perpetrators

1   wish to be allowed to speak again. OK, I
2   will allow you to articulate what is on your
3   mind, and then that will be the end of all
4   of this, except for the verdict and then
5   sentencing.
6
7
8   **JUDGE:** Yes, at the time of your criminal
9   activities, whether individually or jointly,
10   by **THE LAW** spoken, known, and
11   understood by these Defendants, I have no
12   choice but to fulfill the penalty
13   requirements for your actions and inactions.
14
15
16   This is a tragic situation, and the
17   consequences have placed untold future
18   generations in dismal straits. However, it is
19   the inclination of this Court to show
20   leniency in this matter.
21
22
23   (The Prosecutor is showing signs of
24   astonishment)
25
26
27   **PROSECUTOR**: Your Honor?
28
29
30   **JUDGE:** Prosecutor, do you have anything
31   to say? If so, now is the time.

1   **PROSECUTOR:** I want to reiterate that the
2   only penalty permissible is DEATH!
3
4
5   **JUDGE:** Thank you. Now then, ADAM,
6   what more needs to be said that may
7   persuade Me to pronounce a sentence other
8   than what the law allows and calls for?
9
10
11   **ADAM:** I don't believe that I should be
12   sentenced to death, even though I have no
13   idea what that means. I think I should get
14   what You said, Sir, a sentence of leniency.
15   Thank you.
16
17
18   **JUDGE:** Defendant #2, Eve, you may now
19   speak your peace.
20
21
22   **EVE:** Your Honor, thank You for another
23   opportunity to speak. As a woman, the
24   weaker of the two flesh beings, I believe
25   I am entitled to the leniency You spoke of a
26   moment ago.
27
28
29   Like ADAM, I do not know what death is.
30   It sounds scary to say the least, Sir.
31

1   I don't want any sentence that will cause me
2   to suffer more than I have so far, so please
3   consider not only leniency, but also the
4   pardon mentioned earlier.
5
6   Thank You again, Sir.
7

8

9   **JUDGE:** You motioned for a chance to
10   speak as well, SERPENT, so let Me hear it.
11

12

13   **SERPENT:** (Smiling devilishly) Sir, I still
14   claim innocence. Also, I agree with Your
15   pronouncement of leniency, especially in
16   my case.
17

18

19   I did not commit the crime that ADAM and
20   EVE committed, and I did not cause either
21   one to do anything they had not thought of
22   before acting on their own. I think that…
23

24

25   **JUDGE:** I AM tired of hearing your lies!
26   Be quiet! Speak no more forever in an
27   understandable voice!
28

29

30   (Though the SERPENT continues to speak,
31   no sound comes out of his mouth.)

1   **JUDGE:** The first to be sentenced will be
2   the SERPENT.
3
4
5   The verdict will be fair and just. You
6   willingly participated in the crimes
7   committed by these Defendants, ADAM
8   and EVE, by your insistent talking and the
9   cunning ways in which you twisted words.
10
11
12 Leniency is extended to Defendants 1 and 2,
13 but not for you. Your actions and omissions
14 prescribe a different sentence. Your sentences
15 will be imposed and enforced today. Look
16 long and hard at ADAM and EVE, for they
17 are going to be able to restrain you.
18
19
20 (Adam and Eve exchange smiles, and now
21 think, "this just might work in their favor"
22 and they might indeed get a break.)
23
24
25 **JUDGE:** You shall no longer have the
26 ability to speak in a voice that is heard or
27 understood by mankind or any other
28 living creature.
29
30
31 And, Serpent, you shall no longer stand but

1   forever crawl upon your belly, eating the
2   dust of the ground because of your
3   deceitfulness. This sentence will be a
4   never–ending reminder of this day, and it
5   will be an everlasting sign to all who see
6   you and your kind.
7
8
9   Your body will now start to reform itself.
10   Your legs are disappearing. Your voice has
11   already been forever silenced.
12
13
14   (THE SERPENT's mouth continues to move,
15   but no sound is heard. He begins to sink to
16   the ground beneath him, and he starts to
17   wiggle instead of walking on the ground.)
18
19
20   **JUDGE:** You will eat the dust of the earth
21   forever, and you will learn to enjoy it. This
22   rebuke addresses your intentional trickery.
23
24
25   Crawling upon your belly is for your
26   cunning manner. Then, when the end of time
27   has come, you will forever be banned from
28   all of creation, as you are now banned from
29   the Garden of Eden.
30
31

1   (THE SERPENT starts slithering off,
2   and then raises his head to continue
3   listening.)
4
5
6   **JUDGE:** The leniency I am extending
7   to you will not last forever. I AM
8   formulating a plan to reconcile those
9   who will be born after this fatal day.
10 You will not be able to mislead those
11 who accept and receive the Eternal Life
12 Salvation Package for they will live
13 forever in the heavenlies with those who
14 make it in before the last day comes to
15 pass. ADAM, EVE, the Garden of Eden,
16 and everything within it – the Earth and
17 the fullness thereof – are MY Creation,
18 and you will never have total control
19 again!
20
21
22 (THE SERPENT lays his head down
23 and slithers out of the courtroom and
24 out of God's sight.)
25
26
27 **JUDGE:** Now it is your turn, ADAM.
28 I have heard your testimony, and
29 considered your criminal acts and
30 omissions. It is time to deliver My
31 verdict and impose the sentence you

1   have coming, which is death.

2

3

4   A "Death Sentence" is a permanent

5   punishment, and the only permissible

6   consequence for your knowing and willful

7   participation in and disobedience of the Law

8   you plainly understood.

9

10

11   (EVE gloats. ADAM's mouth drops open in

12   disbelief, and he hangs his head.)

13

14

15   **JUDGE:** However, ADAM, you will also

16   obtain leniency.

17

18

19   (ADAM looks hopefully at GOD. But EVE

20   is confused)

21

22

23   Eve starts thinking,

24

25   What is – Death – and –

26

27   What is – Leniency?"

28

29   What does Death look like?

30

31   What is this thing called leniency, and how

1   can that be good for me, Adam, and the
2   Serpent?
3
4
5   I am so scared because I don't understand
6   any of this.)
7
8
9   **JUDGE:** It is leniency I am giving you in
10   the death sentence, ADAM. No longer will
11   you dwell in the Garden of Eden nor will
12   you be allowed to see, touch, or taste fruits
13   of any tree in the Garden of Eden
14   ever again.
15
16
17   ADAM, your separation from Me and My
18   presence eternally is the death sentence of
19   which I speak. This is the first of your
20   punishments.
21
22
23   (Adam cannot believe there is more. He
24   opens his mouth to interrupt, but his defeat
25   is so complete that he is unable to utter a
26   sound.)
27
28
29   **JUDGE:** You have also lost the right to be
30   ruler over and to subdue the Earth. This
31   punishment rectifies your crime, that is

1   known as the act of omission.
2
3
4   The fact is that you did nothing to stop or
5   prevent EVE from touching, holding, and
6   tasting the Forbidden Fruit. Neither did you
7   stop the SERPENT from speaking to and
8   tempting EVE. You are fully responsible
9   for both of their actions.
10
11
12   You demonstrated that you cannot be trusted
13   to perform your duties as ruler.
14
15
16   Another punishment I am imposing upon
17   you is the bittersweet fruit of remembrance.
18   You will suffer anguish when you
19   contemplate what you had, could now have,
20   and what you willingly lost because of your
21   actions and omissions. You are eternally
22   banned from Paradise, the place prepared
23   for your joint habitation.
24
25
26   (ADAM's thoughts go back to the beauty he
27   saw daily in the Garden of Eden. He
28   desperately searches his mind for something
29   to say that would give him another chance to
30   return to the Garden of Eden and obey
31   the Law.)

1   **JUDGE:** Other penalties, ADAM, will be
2   that you will come to know what it means
3   to be tired. You will work hard in the heat
4   of the day, tilling the ground for food. You
5   have never known what it is to sweat, but
6   now you will. You will feel the coolness
7   of the evening, and desire EVE to keep
8   you warm. You will physically die, and
9   your body shall return to the earth,
10 becoming dust, for that is from what you
11 were made, and to dust you will certainly
12 return. These are fair and just punishments
13 for your entanglement and disobedience.
14
15
16 ADAM: (Angrily) Your Honor, there was
17 no way I could stop EVE from admiring,
18 desiring, touching, picking, holding and
19 finally tasting – I meant to say EATING –
20 the Forbidden Fruit. In fact, EVE, the one
21 **YOU** made for me, ate first.
22
23
24 After I watched for a little while, and she
25 did not change in anyway, I accepted the
26 fruit she offered me. It is her fault for
27 tricking me with her eyes and the beautiful
28 smile that I love and adore. I never asked
29 YOU to give me a partner for my sadness,
30 which you called loneliness.
31

1   Sir, if I may be so bold, YOU took it upon
2   Yourself to make her, give her to me, and
3   place her in the Paradise that YOU claim to
4   have made for me.
5
6
7   **JUDGE:** Enough, ADAM, enough!
8   I require your silence for the remainder of
9   these proceedings.
10
11
12   You are to stand there and hear the fate you
13   willingly brought upon yourself. Your
14   actions and your acts of omission have
15   brought this sentence upon you. You will
16   serve it in its entirety. I have allowed your
17   vain pleadings, ADAM, but they have not
18   swayed Me.
19
20
21   Did I create EVE for you? Yes, ADAM,
22   I did. Did I cause you to accept the fruit
23   from her hand?
24
25   Absolutely not! So, tell Me, ADAM, what
26   was it that I personally did to help the
27   SERPENT, EVE, or yourself to commit
28   these crimes? How am I at fault?
29
30   Did you seriously think that you could
31   change the penalty for rebelling against

1   the **Law**? Nothing will change the facts: you,
2   of your own accord, willfully and knowingly
3   sinned against "My Commandments."
4
5
6   ADAM, you do not even realize that your
7   sin was the sin of LOVE! Yes, ADAM, you
8   lost your "first love" – your love, desire,
9   and passion for ME – love that was holy and
10   without blame.
11
12
13   (GOD's eyes show His extreme sorrow over
14   the loss of ADAM's love.)
15
16
17   **JUDGE:** ADAM, you chose to give your
18   love to EVE. Yes, I made Eve for you to
19   love, and to replace the loneliness in your
20   heart with a mate who is equal to you and
21   for you. But, I also gave you the ability to
22   love Me more than you love EVE. The one
23   you loved, desired, and longed to stay with
24   eternally was EVE, not Me.
25
26
27   The sentence I have imposed will remain as
28   pronounced in this court today!
29
30
31   (Tears silently flow down ADAM's face.)

1   **ADAM:** Why do I have to pay so much
2   more of a penalty than THE SERPENT?
3   Your Honor, if it had not been for EVE's
4   disobedient actions, I would not be here
5   listening to You give me the worst possible
6   sentence. She handed me the fruit. I never
7   touched it until SHE came along. I didn't
8   want to be rude to her, Sir, so I just took a
9   very, very small bite (demonstrating with
10 his fingers). In all actuality, Sir, the bite I
11 took was nowhere near the size of EVE's.
12 Her bite (using both hands) was enormous.
13
14
15 (GOD rises to His full stature, towering over
16 ADAM.)
17
18 **JUDGE:** I will hear no more from you!
19 There is NO further negotiating or pleading.
20 Your sentence has been imposed, and you
21 have been found guilty. Your punishment is
22 for the way you acted and for your failure
23 to act.
24
25
26 Your sentence will begin today, for surely
27 this day you have been tried and weighed in
28 the balance of justice, and you have been
29 found wanting. Now, ADAM, be gone from
30 My presence.
31

1   (ADAM hangs his head in shame and

2   disbelief, vanishing as he does so.)

3

4

5   (EVE starts to feel fear, something she

6   never knew before. She inwardly

7   rationalizes that GOD will give her more

8   leniency than He did Adam since he was the

9   authorized ruler over all living things in the

10   Garden of Eden. Satisfied with her

11   reasoning, she smiles with confidence. GOD

12   might even say I am innocent, deliberately

13   deceived by the craftiness of the SERPENT,

14   she thinks.)

15

16

17   **JUDGE:** EVE, I am just, as you have seen

18   and heard.

19

20

21   I will now show you leniency, as I showed

22   ADAM and the SERPENT. You heard

23   their sentences, EVE, and your penalty

24   cannot be anything other than the same

25   penalty – death. This penalty, although you

26   may not agree, is lenient.

27

28

29   (She is shaken but believes she will not be

30   punished further.)

31

1 **JUDGE:** The sentence I've spoken and
2 imposed upon you is permanent. It is the
3 consequence of your willful, knowing, and
4 intentional disobedience.
5
6
7 You knew the penalty ahead of time and yet
8 chose to blatantly ignore it.
9
10
11 Another punishment is that ADAM will
12 now rule over you. You will no longer be
13 ADAM's equal.
14
15
16 You will desire him and want to be with him
17 for many reasons. And when you give birth,
18 your discomfort and birth pains will be
19 multiplied. And you, too, will know anxiety
20 and anguish forever.
21
22
23 You will remember the pain and discomfort
24 of giving birth. When you see the face of the
25 child you have brought into this world, you
26 will be reminded of these proceedings
27 because you, Eve, brought the sin they will
28 be born with through your willful
29 disobedience and your blatant lack of
30 concern for your offspring and their future
31 generations as well.

1   All of this is your fault and Adam's fault.
2   Adam could have done more to prevent
3   you from listening to the Serpent, talking
4   with the Serpent, desiring the forbidden
5   fruit, and more.
6
7
8   EVE, you chose to do what your husband,
9   ADAM, told you I did not want either of
10 you to do at the forbidden fruit tree.
11
12 (EVE speaks arrogantly.)
13
14 **EVE:** Excuse me? Your Honor, the
15 SERPENT tricked me, And ADAM did not
16 protect me, which was his obligation and
17 duty. There is no way that I am so guilty as
18 to receive the harshest punishments! I
19 certainly should receive more compassion
20 and greater leniency than either ADAM or
21 the SERPENT. I throw myself upon the
22 mercies of this Honorable Court and You,
23 GOD!
24
25
26 **JUDGE:** EVE, say no more. Believe me
27 when I tell you I AM showing you leniency.
28
29
30 Your pleading will not sway My decision.
31 Your sentence stands as it was pronounced.

1   You, too, shall sweat in the heat of the day
2   and feel the chill of the evenings. When you
3   feel this cold, you will desire the comfort
4   and companionship of ADAM for warmth
5   and protection.
6
7
8   You will have intense knowledge of sorrow,
9   fear, weariness, worry, hunger, and thirst.
10 These punishments are because of your
11 willing and active participation in your
12 crimes.
13
14
15 Now and forever, EVE, you are banned
16 from the Paradise I created for you, the
17 Garden of Eden. But the greatest
18 punishment is this: you will be forever
19 separated from My Presence.
20
21
22 These punishments are a total Death
23 Sentence package. Now, go away, EVE,
24 and be with ADAM until physical death
25 overtakes you.
26
27
28 Be Gone!
29
30
31 (EVE opens her mouth to speak and, like

1   Adam, evaporates.)

2

3

4   (The Judge now addresses the spectators in

5   the courtroom)

6

7

8   ADAM, EVE, and THE SERPENT tried to

9   accuse Me of being party to the criminal

10   actions that they individually and

11   corporately committed.

12

13

14   Before this entire courtroom, I declare that

15   I AM not guilty in any way of any crime

16   or misconduct.

17

18

19   "I AM" the Creator of the solar systems,

20   matter, and energy, planets, stars, suns,

21   moons, and angels, including Lucifer (now

22   known as the SERPENT), of water, animals,

23   plants, and all edible food. I imagined man,

24   and then I created the Garden of Eden and

25   all it contains. And afterwards, I formed

26   ADAM and placed him in the Garden to

27   care for it. I noticed ADAM was lonely,

28   so I caused him to go into a deep sleep.

29

30

31   From his side, I took a piece of rib bone

1   and that's how I created – you – EVE. You
2   were to be his helpmate and partner to cure
3   his loneliness. I also created the Tree of
4   Knowledge of Good and Evil, and other
5   fruit trees located in the Garden of Eden.
6
7
8   The Defendants in today's trial ate
9   forbidden fruit from that tree. I created that
10   specific tree – the Tree of Knowledge of
11   Good And Evil – and yes, the fruit
12   contained both good and evil. Neither
13   ADAM nor EVE was to partake of the
14   forbidden fruit which that tree produced.
15
16
17   Yes, Good and Evil are equal and equally
18   important.
19
20
21   We must have a Positive if we have a
22   Negative, an Up as well as a Down. In other
23   words, it's what we do with The Good
24   and... or The Evil that determines the
25   greatest significance to us.
26
27
28   The "Good AND Evil" was self–contained
29   within the confines of "The Forbidden Fruit."
30   The only way for evil to manifest was
31   through mankind's disobedience

to **The Law.**

I created ALL things to be good. I gave
ADAM and EVE the choice, the free will
to decide for themselves by their actions,
words, and beliefs. Because of
disobedience, the infection (sin) of evil
dispersed and entered their bodies. It will
continue through their offspring. Both
chose to do the wrong thing.

I made the Garden pleasant for them. I love
EVE just as much as I love ADAM. My
hands made them, and I gave them life.
I have love for them still, but I despise the
sin that now resides within them; therefore,
they will be living examples destined to
change the hearts and minds of future
generations.

Know this: "There is a plan!"

I have set forth a plan and put it in place to
resolve the outcome of ADAM and EVE's
failure. It is the greatest sacrifice I will ever
make.

The greatest sacrifice of all time, and it will
be carried out by My beloved Son.

1   Coming to earth in the flesh, He will be and
2   bring the only cure for sin that you three –
3   ADAM, EVE, and SERPENT – have
4   unleashed upon the Earth.
5
6   I want to thank everyone in attendance today
7   for their time and silence. This is a very
8   delicate and terrible case to listen to, and it
9   makes Me feel sad to have brought this case
10   before the entire host of heavenly angels,
11   and before the Defendants, ADAM and EVE.
12   They did not know that the SERPENT was
13   corrupt before he ever spoke a word to them.
14   The SERPENT will be sentenced in front of
15   ADAM and EVE so they get to know more
16   about him.
17
18   The court is closing this case. I now speak to
19   each Defendant so they know what
20   My decision is.
21
22
23   **Judge:** SERPENT! You are being sentenced
24   as a Habitual Offender! This means you are
25   a repeat criminal lawbreaker.
26
27   You will be sentenced to Hell, and that will
28   include the Lake of Fire, which will never
29   be extinguished.
30
31   You are hideous and spiteful, to say the least.

Your intentions to destroy My perfect
Garden, and ADAM, EVE, and their
children are despicable. You AND your
band of fallen angels will spend eternity
in the lowest part of Earth.

"Habitual Offender" is just one of your
sentences. You are also being sentenced to
"eternity" in hell. You will not be alone
because those angels who left heaven to
follow you and your plans will join you in
a place not meant for anyone else.

Human beings will be "intruders" of this
realm if they live and die without accepting
"the cure" for sin, Salvation, known as
Redemption, through My Son.

Goodbye to you forever. I will make sure
that you never get to keep the trophy, the
"birthright" to the Garden of Eden and to
the souls of ADAM and EVE.

JUDGE: ADAM, I am sentencing you to
"Death," but with "Leniency" included.

The death you are getting starts now.
Let Me explain what this death is, so you
have a better understanding of its meaning.

The Death I speak of is your separation

1   from Me. When you were able to walk and
2   talk with Me daily, that was life to you.
3   You will not get to walk and talk with Me
4   face to face again. If you accept "the cure"
5   for sin from My Son, you will have an
6   opportunity to live and abide in Heaven
7   with family members, and friends.
8
9
10   Yes, you will have an opportunity to be
11   reconciled with Me again. However, until
12   the opportunity comes, you will have to
13   endure feelings associated with death.
14   You will have the opportunity to once
15   again be free from the strongholds that
16   will bind you: sin, death, and hell.
17
18
19   As part of the sentences imposed on you
20   today, ADAM, you will learn how to sweat
21   from the heat of the day and the labor of
22   your hands. You will learn how to cope
23   with the cold, which will cause great
24   discomfort.
25
26   ADAM, you will experience pain so
27   intensely that you will seek relief from
28   herbs, plants, doctors, and others. Your life
29   will be more difficult than it was meant to
30   be for you, your wife, your children, and
31   your grandchildren.

1   **JUDGE:** EVE, it's time to announce your
2   punishments. You knew not to do what you
3   so willingly chose to do. Your actions
4   violated what you knew to be true. Adam
5   told you that I did not want either of you to
6   partake of the forbidden fruit on the Tree
7   of Knowledge of Good And Evil.
8
9
10   Yes, the fruit was pretty to see. Yes, the fruit
11   was contained within the confines of its
12   specially created surroundings. You didn't
13   know, and you still don't know what
14   "to die" means, but you will know very well
15   what it means after this trial today.
16
17
18   EVE, because you risked touching the
19   forbidden fruit and tasting it, and you
20   offered it to your husband to eat and taste,
21   I have no choice but to impose and enforce
22   the sentence that is known as DEATH upon
23   you. As I said to your husband, you will
24   know this new feeling quite well.
25
26
27   Since you will be on the outside – trying to
28   look in – to the Garden of Eden, you will
29   remember how good you had it, but you
30   cannot go back. You have done this to
31   yourself, and you will cry inwardly and

outwardly for your loss. You will remember
what you did, and you will always be
miserable because of the choices you made.

Far in the future, someone named Cher will
record a song that says:

"If I could turn back time."

That will be a constant thought, but one
day, just like your husband, you will have
a chance to accept "the cure" for the sin
you two allowed to infiltrate your body,
mind, heart, and spirit.

You will show outward signs of shame to
those with whom you come in contact. You
must live with the memory of these things,
EVE.

Your saving hope is when "The Gift of
Redemption" is offered to you and others.
This gift will be free to whomever will
accept it, but it will cost Me more than
you could ever imagine. It will involve
a one–time sacrifice, and it will be called
"Salvation."

1   It will come solely through My Son and His
2   Sacrifice for ALL of Mankind.
3
4   You will not be able to tell anyone what the
5   inside of The Garden of Eden looked like.
6
7   You will not be able to bring anyone to Me.
8
9   You cannot experience inner peace because
10   you will never know true peace until and
11   unless you accept My Son's sacrifice, which
12   is called: **Salvation**.

The transcript section ended.

Don't worry, more books are coming in this Redemption
Collection.

This is the first part of a three–part trilogy.

This is book number one of a three–part series.

Here are some questions in Volume 1 and Volume 2, which I call

They will be answered in the next two books

1. **Was the Tree of Knowledge of Good and Evil a real tree or something else?**

2. **Was the Forbidden Fruit real fruit as we know fruit to be, or was the fruit something else?**

3. **Was the serpent really a snake or something else?**

4. **Why was Eve created from Adam's rib?**

5. **Did Adam have an extra rib or did he lose one in order for God to create Eve?**

6   **Do women have more ribs than men?**

And other questions that have been asked, I will expound on.

Those questions and more will be answered in books two and three:

Book 2 – **"The Genesis Effect"**

Book 3 – **"The Blood Sealing Covenant"**

I started book 4, and I gave it a name. But God may change its name before it's published. I don't have a problem with God doing that.

Book 4 – **"The Fruit and Their Purpose for US"**

Their titles so far are:

"The Greatest Gift Ever Given"

ALL of my books are "God-inspired"

"From Rejection To Acceptance"

This is a honest–to–God true story of my life. To disclose a story about your life isn't easy because you relive the incidents that repeatedly happened to you, and who the perpetrators were that did the dirty deed(s). The emotions felt then sometimes resurface. Through God's grace and professional counseling, we can be set free and delivered from all the effects of a lifelong horrendous life with lots of experiences.

Like "THE TRIAL" this is not something to read for people with weak stomachs. Nothing will be in great detail, but you will be able to read between the lines enough to know what happened. Some of the people I will not mention their real name. Why? Because some of them passed away, and I don't want to tarnish their reputation.

I pray that each book will bring someone closer to God and help others by enlightenment. People are always asking to divulge information, and while answering their questions could be a good thing, it can also cause great despair in the lives of family members and friends who would not believe that the person mentioned did what I say. You may have a tough time with some of the things I write in my personal life book.

Footnotes that did not get included in the writings above.

¹ **Genesis 2:16-17 (16)** "And the LORD God commanded the man, saying, 'Of every tree of the garden thou mayest freely eat: **(17)** But of the tree of the knowledge of good and evil, thou shalt not eat of it: for in the day that thou eatest thereof thou shalt surely die.'"

² **Genesis 3:2-3 (2)** "And the woman said unto the serpent, 'We may eat of the fruit of the trees of the garden: **(3)** But of the fruit of the tree which is in the midst of the garden, God hath said, Ye shall not eat of it, neither shall ye touch it, lest ye die.'"

³ DEATH for Adam and Eve differs from the serpent. Adam and Eve did not have, due to their flawless design and formation (without sin), our sinful conception and birth. Thus, death for the serpent and his followers would – permanently – impede any reconciliation.

EPILOGUE

The court proceedings, transcripts, and trial were created primarily for the purpose of entertainment. More importantly, they were also created to stretch our understanding of the changes wrought in Adam, Eve, the serpent, and future inhabitants of Earth. The transcripts are not to be considered authentic. They are my version of the charges, procedures, and proceedings brought against the participants, and heard in and before the Presence of God. Now I ask you to continue our journey to explore the effects of the choices Adam and Eve knowingly and willingly made.

Many people want to learn and try to uncover the hidden secrets of God and "the beginning." The Bible introduces us in (Genesis 1:1) to time and creation. Information is also recorded in the fourth book of the New Testament, the Gospel of John. In fact, both books open with the same three words: "In the beginning…." I firmly believe God wanted us to know <u>there was</u> a beginning to everything created. Another book in the Old Testament, Ecclesiastes, backs my statement. If you read the third chapter, I believe you will see there was and there is "a time" or beginning, to all things. In the same way, there will be an ending to all things. Again, if there's a positive, there has to be a negative. If there's good, evil also exists. And, if there is a starting place, there must be an ending place. God and His Word, the Holy Bible, are infallible!

I will be the first to admit that I do not know all, or even enough (yet) of the secrets within God's Word. I certainly would like to know more, but until God gives me the answers, I will not trust another man or woman who claims to have the answer.

ALL of the secrets and truths locked away within the sixty– six (66) books of the King James Version Bible are equally important. To me, the most important of all the secrets concerns creation. God has given me some unusual perspectives. I am not a theologian, scientist, or seminary student/graduate; I have studied the Word of God and hold a Theological Doctorate Degree in Biblical Studies. I am nothing without Him ruling and reigning in my life each moment. If I were not a willing vessel, I would be hopeless. However, I have been blessed with an ability to preach, teach, and deliver some inside tidbits from "**the author and finisher**" (of my faith), God Almighty.

Have you really taken time to contemplate how magnificent the Garden of Eden must have been and how uncomplicated life was? My research indicates the Garden was more beautiful than we could ever imagine in our wildest thoughts and dreams. Note, if you will, the underlined words of mine used in the last verse of Genesis, Chapter One: **"And God saw every thing that he had made, and, behold, it was <u>very good</u>. And the evening and the morning were the sixth day."**

The combination of these two words – very good – has a far deeper and richer meaning than we usually realize. When we combine them, they mean **"extraordinary."** The Garden of Eden, if we could see it after its creation, would be so awe–inspiring that nothing could sway us from making the choice to be **Christians** (Christ–Followers) just to have the opportunity to live in this paradise one day. Try to imagine all the colors. Flowers are everywhere, always in full bloom, with fragrances we've never smelled before. The best smell you can imagine isn't even close to the aromatic beauty of this handmade Garden.

In book two – **"The Genesis Effect"** – there's one chapter that you may find humorous, for I titled it **"Why, Adam, Why?"** In it, I attempt to get into Adam's mind to discover a reason WHY he accepted and ate the Forbidden Fruit Eve offered to him. Adam and Eve, in making the decisions they did caused us to suffer for their disobedience. Yet the greatest part is that we have an opportunity to be disease–free when we accept the blood sacrifice of Jesus as our substitutionary debt cancellation. We were and are, until the rapturing away of His People, infected with inherited but curable sin. Have you ever thought about the word disease? Notice it is two words in combination. It is good when you're at ease, right? But when something comes along to rock your boat, so to speak, it becomes **dis**ease. Don't let the enemy be the one to rock your boat. Let God be the Captain of your ship, and you'll make it to safe harbor.

DISease is nothing more than being uncomfortable or infected, if you will, by the cares of this life: circumstances, losing a loved one, a child being sick, etc. However, God said, and I believe it to be a fact, nothing will be placed upon us that we are unable to handle or are ill–equipped to battle through as we access His Power, Mercy, and Grace.

Another topic for reflection is the **death sentence** Adam and Eve received. God insists that this penalty is lenient, but to our natural mind, that is a contradiction. He had the right and the ability to kill them then and there, but He let them live – just not in the Garden. So, then, how did they receive the death penalty? Adam and Eve lost their right to be and participate in the Presence of God, as well as losing their right to the eternal life that was provided by the Creator of Everything. We are the only creatures made by God's hands who have gone astray. (Most people do not know that God spoke **Lucifer** into existence – **Ezekiel 28:15**). And still, God had a plan to restore the lost attributes of Adam and Eve. He sent us His best gift, who is none other than the Lord Jesus, who obediently sacrificed His mortal body, allowing it to be nailed to the cross. His obedience to the will of God was (and is) a witness – an example – for us to follow. He died on that cross and was buried in a (borrowed) stone tomb. On the third day, He was restored to life and was seen by hundreds of people. He walked through walls and ate food. He was tested by one of His disciples, Thomas, who doubted what he saw and heard, just as we would have. Jesus proved to those who would serve Him in Spirit and in Truth that He was (is) God's Son, the Alpha and Omega. Together these acts – His death and His resurrection – redeemed our relationship with God, and He returned our rightfully intended eternal life. However, eternal life no longer comes automatically; we must believe in and accept Jesus Christ as our Savior, living a life of active faith.

Think back to your childhood. I believe you can recall at least one time when chastisement was administered because of disobedience. You were likely punished out of love, even though you might not have thought you were wrong. As you grew up, it should have become obvious that, in most cases, when you did get punished, it was to teach you right from wrong, good from bad. This knowledge, achieved through reflection, is a key factor in gaining wisdom. So, it was with Adam and Eve and the portion of their sentence where God dictates, they will sorrowfully reflect on their crimes and their losses. This reflection was intended to be a method of instruction for the acquisition of wisdom. We make that same journey.

Book Two
of this series is
"The Genesis Effect"

Everything in life has a purpose and a reason. As we travel down the path of life, it is our quest – in the way we were designed – to discover, seek, find, and to reason why just as Adam and Eve did "… in the beginning…."

As I close, I don't want you to forget what you read in the Trial Transcripts. Examine how you feel now about these important chapters of Genesis. Do you think differently about the Garden of Eden, our lost Paradise? Do you find yourself in Adam, Eve, or even the Serpent? Do you have questions about the Tree of Knowledge of Good And Evil, and its Forbidden Frui? Can you imagine the dialogues between Eve and the Serpent, Adam and the Serpent? Have you ever imagined what it must have been like when they stood before God, clothed by His very hand compared to their previous **unashamed, fearless nakedness**?

Did you see or read anything that answered some of your questions about Adam and Eve's banishment? If you still have unanswered questions, more books are coming in which you may find some answers to the questions you have pondered and asked without getting a satisfactory reply.

We will never know all the answers! Sometimes the answers we seek are not meant to be uncovered. In fact, if we knew all the answers to everything, we wouldn't be mortal beings and we wouldn't need God.

As a follower of God's Son, Jesus, you will come to believe "The Word of God" (the Holy Bible) to be God's inspired words to and for us, and you will have and hold **ALL the answers** to questions you wondered about and asked. The humorous part of that is: in heaven, you will not even remember wonder about and ponder here on earth usually cause us pain and discomfort. All the questions and events that cause us hurt and sorrow will not be a part of our reality when we live for all eternity with God. Isn't that wonderful?

Book Three

of this series is

"The Blood Sealing Covenant"

The Blood Sealing Covenant demonstrates how God made and gave the first covenant mentioned in the Holy Bible, and that covenant is everlasting. Isn't that wonderful? Do not get it wrong, please. God does not covet, but He covers His children with an everlasting covenant. God's covenant cannot be broken or taken away by anyone other than God. A covenant between man and God can be lost because mankind makes mistakes. Only God can make a covenant that cannot be broken or taken by our enemy, the father of lies, satan, lucifer, the evil one, etc.

Men make covenants between themselves, but we get busy, forget and cancel the covenant by not following through on what we agreed to do. We stop giving what we agreed to give. We simply stop showing up. Mankind's covenants cannot compare to God's covenant. Though we may intend to be honest and abide by our "covenant" to another, we almost always fall short on completing our "word". We are faulty but thank God that HE IS NOT ever remiss with any of the covenants He has offered and given to us.

I look forward to hearing your thoughts, questions, and comments on any of my books in this "Redemption Series."